God Is . . .

God Is . . .

Meditations on the Mystery of Life, the Purity of Grace,
the Bliss of Surrender, and the God beyond God

Rev. Dr. Wesley J. Wildman
Boston University

CASCADE *Books* · Eugene, Oregon

GOD IS . . .
Meditations on the Mystery of Life, the Purity of Grace, the Bliss of Surrender, and the God beyond God

Copyright © 2019 Wesley J. Wildman. All rights reserved. Except for brief quotations in critical publications or reviews, no part of this book may be reproduced in any manner without prior written permission from the publisher. Write: Permissions, Wipf and Stock Publishers, 199 W. 8th Ave., Suite 3, Eugene, OR 97401.

Cascade Books
An Imprint of Wipf and Stock Publishers
199 W. 8th Ave., Suite 3
Eugene, OR 97401

www.wipfandstock.com

PAPERBACK ISBN: 978-1-5326-5919-5
HARDCOVER ISBN: 978-1-5326-5920-1
EBOOK ISBN: 978-1-5326-5921-8

Cataloguing-in-Publication data:

Names: Wildman, Wesley, J., author. | Hill, Robert Allen, foreword.
Title: God is . . . : meditations on the mystery of life, the purity of grace, the bliss of surrender, and the God beyond God / by Wesley J. Wildman; foreword by Robert Allen Hill.
Description: Eugene, OR : Cascade Books, 2019
Identifiers: ISBN 978-1-5326-5919-5 (paperback) | ISBN 978-1-5326-5920-1 (hardcover) | ISBN 978-1-5326-5921-8 (ebook)
Subjects: LCSH: God (Christianity). | Sermons, American. | Life—Religious aspects—Sermons. | Grace (Theology)—Sermons.
Classification: LCC E185.9.M6 C58 2018 (print) | LCC E185.9.M6 (ebook)

Manufactured in the U.S.A.

Dedicated to Boston University's Marsh Chapel and
the host of its pulpit's astonishingly varied occupants

Contents

Foreword ix
Preface xvii
The Sermons xix
A Prayer before Each Sermon xxi

God Is . . . Holy Mystery 1
God Is . . . Friend 9
God Is . . . Hope 21
God Is . . . Monarch 30
God Is . . . Wisdom 37
God Is . . . Coming 45
God Is . . . Death 54
God Is . . . Creator 63
God Is . . . Waiting 72

Foreword

By Rev. Dr. Robert Allen Hill, Dean of Marsh Chapel, Boston University

PROFESSOR WESLEY WILDMAN HERE offers students, colleagues, fellow preachers and teachers, and the wider reading public, a selection and collection of his sermons, a most welcome offering. The nine sermons here assembled he identifies as "meditations," following on the Scripture texts on which they were based. In that spirit, we too might want to meditate on the sermons herein, especially as they provide insight and perspective with regard to the gospel and truth, with regard to Scripture and the preaching tradition, and with regard to designs for preaching.

Professor Wildman's sermons, to begin with, challenge us and cause us to meditate carefully on what we judge to be true, the truth the whole truth and nothing but the truth, about God and the gospel. Not long ago, for instance, a vigorous debate emerged about the importance of going to church. The initial proposition affirming required attendance in worship and the spiritual centrality of worship, the judgment that for the Christian person worship is not optional, came from a group who emphasized the healing and healthy social aspects of worship. A sense of belonging kindles a sense of meaning, which develops into community and issues into a feeling of empowerment. It is good to go to church, for there you find friends, thoughts, intimacy and strength. One does well to affirm all of this, and one has a hard time denying any of it.

But from another corner, during this recent debate, came voices in opposition: One said, *I do go to church, and I do value belonging, meaning, community and empowerment. I am a better person for having prayed,*

Foreword

sung, listened, gathered, and given. However, in the long run, many of us, perhaps most of us, will not continue to attend if we judge what we hear, in preaching, is not based on solid theology and philosophy. Another similarly responded, *It is tempting to disjoin learning and vital piety, but it is not loving or wise to disjoin learning and vital piety. They go together. The God of Creation is the very God of Redemption. Their disjunction may help us cling for a while to a kind of faux certainty. But their conjunction is the confidence born of obedience.* A sermon collection like the one you are now holding, entering, and soon reading, reminds you of your childhood in creation and redemption. Not your youthful past but your childhood: You are a child of God. Howard Thurman famously concluded his masterpiece, *Jesus and the Disinherited*, with just this thought. To allow such gracious sensibility to live, though, requires all the heavy thought and truth telling we can muster, in preaching. A laywoman from California, Judith Mang, in a 2008 *New York Times* letter to the editor, put it this way: "It is likely that nothing will match the reassurance of a Sunday morning spent in church. But for an ever-growing number of Americans, the conviction that the church is built on shaky philosophical grounds is more powerful than the longing for unconditional comfort." The two, learning and piety, perhaps in the long run cannot finally be disjoined. Nor can the religious longing ever easily be written out of human life: whatever introduces genuine perspective is itself religious, to paraphrase John Dewey.

Professor Wesley Wildman has compiled a welcome collection of sermons meant to advance genuine religious perspective and to address the issue of shaky philosophical foundations. His sermons, from various angles of vision, and out of a variety of moments in Scripture and experience, together raise a challenge for the contemporary preacher. Do you believe what you are about to say, in all its complexity and opacity? Is what you are saying reasonable? Are the words taken from tradition and Scripture, and lifted in preaching, "good tradition or bad tradition"—"the living faith of dead people or the dead faith of living people" (as Jaroslav Pelikan put it)? Is it true? Better to be too true to be good than to be too good to be true, on this estimate. Better not to use a word at all, unless you are confident of its meaning and of your capacity to convey that meaning in a true, in a reasonable, in a defensible way. Wildman's work affords us the opportunity to meditate upon the gospel and truth.

The sermons here also cause us to meditate on Scripture and traditions. The reader of these nine sermons will soon sense the apophatic inclination

Foreword

of the collection. Yes, there is a struggle with a respect for Scripture, but not a wooden allegiance to revelation in the raw. So too with traditions and experiences, cited but not worshipped for their own sake, much as St. Paul put his faith origin "by revelation" (Gal 1:12) beyond both. At heart, or at bottom, there is here a stark admission that for many things we are in the dark, alone, and will need to do the best we can, working things out for ourselves, by our own best light, however dim. Still, like Paul Tillich before him, Wildman does not abandon Scripture and its outgrowths in history, though his own full understanding of the authority of Scripture is left unstated, meant perhaps to be gleaned directly in the reading of the sermons. He stands in the pulpit, with tradition. He reads from Holy Writ, with inherited custom. He blends his reason and experience with others. He does so at a time when, still, 38% of the US population denies evolution, the origin of species by natural selection through random mutation, in the Darwinian perspective. Wildman will have none of that. What we now know of nature, we now know, and we must move forward in our preaching. The universe is 14 billion years old. The earth is 4.5 billion years old. 500 million years ago, multi-celled organisms appeared in the Cambrian explosion. 400 million years ago, plants sprouted. 370 million years ago, land animals emerged. 230 million years ago, dinosaurs appeared (and disappeared 65 million years ago). 200,000 years ago, hominids arose. Every human being carries sixty new mutations out of six billion cells. Yes, evolution through natural selection by random mutation is a sturdy, robust, reasonable hypothesis. You love the mind, the reason. You love the prospect of learning. You love the life of the mind. You love the Lord with heart and soul and mind. You know that a mind is a terrible thing to waste. You love the reason in the same way that Charles Darwin, a good Anglican, loved the reason. (Marsh Chapel hosted a series of ten sermons on the theme "Darwin and Faith," offered by preachers from around the country, one included here from Professor Wildman ("God is Creator") during the summer of 2009).

In the same way, we might continue to meditate, we cannot preach as if the last 250 years of biblical scholarship, historical critical study of the Bible, have not occurred and have not yielded solid results. They have and they have. Wildman's sermons here give careful attention to this body of work, and several moments of exemplary rendition and interpretation of the Scriptures, understood in historical and critical perspective. So, where we need to admit our unknowing, our wandering within the clouds of unknowing, our origin and destination in the dark, so be it. After all, the psalmist led the way: *Yes, the heavens are telling the glory of God, but so too the firmament proclaims God's handiwork. Yes, day to day pours forth speech, but also, and more so, night to night declares not only speech but knowledge* (Psalm 19). Dr. Ray L. Hart has well exposed this dual healing fulfillment in interpretation in his recent book, *God Being Nothing* (2016). In Wildman's collection, we take note of the reliance on various texts, and the occasional references to other philosophers and theologians who have touched and influenced this preacher. We might especially meditate along the way on his use of Job, the Psalms, Ecclesiastes, Proverbs, other Wisdom passages, and Samuel.

Furthermore, we cannot expect to gain a hearing, to see by grace the assembly of an addressable community, over time, without rigorous attention to form as well as content, to sermon design as well as sermon theme. In fact, these sermons invite us particularly to look hard at sermon design. Professor Wildman's sermons offer exemplary modes of design, an often under-attended aspect of preaching. Meditate as you read on the varieties of form in the design, and on the rhetorical structures of the sermons. They have a great deal to offer both to the younger and to the older preachers among us. They have movement and range. Notice the way the sermon forms and designs advance the gospel affirmations.

In "Mystery," the design is definition: how shall we understand this single word, *mystery*, this phrase, *holy mystery*. Further, the sermonic mode is warning: Words are always inadequate; we tend to trivialize the divine mystery; we need to be aware of the inadequacy of our theological language. Here the author evokes Rudolph Otto and the *Mysterium Tremendum*. We are held in a terrifying tender hand. And, as Ralph Sockman emphasized, using lakeshore imagery, "The larger the body of knowledge, the longer the shoreline of mystery that surrounds it."

In "Friend" the design is the flow of a stream, in which the hospitality of reality discloses itself with vivid concreteness. We must face that we are running the sociopolitical show ourselves. We need not minimize the ravages of the human condition. The price of freedom in the world is extremely high (a similar argument to that of Erich Fromm in his classic, *Escape From Freedom*). To violence this sermon makes multiple, repeated references. The truth is that suffering mostly crushes. Face the rage of the Psalms. Editing our hearts is betrayal.

In "Waiting," the design is a good old two-point sermon. Here are two kinds of waiting: Joy in life and dread before the bizarre lottery of fate, a fine

Foreword

dialectic reminiscent of Helmut Thielecke's "The Waiting God." Wildman affirms, here and elsewhere, "This God is the very Ground of Being, the depth structures and dynamic flows of life, the cosmic Dao and the God beyond God of our beloved mystics. This God waits for the unfolding of nature itself, of our very lives."

In "Hope," the form is a fine, venerable design, yet one sadly far less used today than a generation ago; *not this, not this, not this . . . but that*. Personal transformation, social justice, life after death, and the Kingdom of God are not forgone conclusions. Notice what we and our world are like, first. Here the reader finds one definition of revelation: revelation can be understood as the disclosure of what we are not (and so what we can be) through the experience of what we are in the context of the mysterious, divine depth of our being, in divinely supported space, with both absence and presence (ever a crucial homiletical dialectic). We are not surprised here to have a reference to "the divine incognito" (of Søren Kierkegaard.)

In "Coming," the design is a question, raised and answered: "Ask yourself this." More sermons should perhaps take this form, a question raised and answered, by way of a method of correlation. We are challenged to face what is daunting: disaster, danger, devastation. We are cautioned here to beware of both semi-biblical distortion and semi-biblical fiction—different misrepresentations of God. We are admonished here to abide by the First Commandment. God's coming is multifaceted and hard to pin down. We need a more robust theism, so that "we can love more truly, live more simply, care more deeply, fight more fairly" (a choice phrase if ever there was one).

In "Monarch," the design is intended to follow the text, though not in a rigidly exegetical sense. Here, as often elsewhere in the sermons, there is a primary emphasis and reliance on the Hebrew Scripture, in its layers of interpretation, from the voice of Samuel, to the shaping of the narrator, to the editing of the redactor. Here we are reminded of the importance of institutions (such an immediately timely word), with a reference to Reinhold Niebuhr and Christian realism. The Divine monarchy relativizes all others. Christ the King is the *only* King. Institutions! You can't live with or without them! Here as so often in the sermons there is steady emphasis on dialectical thought and expression.

In "Wisdom," the design, the rhetorical movement, is from similar to different, from familiar to less familiar, relying on Psalm 19 and Proverbs 1. The sermon begins with playful references to dozens of English words for "fool." Here is a good, direct sermonic reminder, for the preacher, to engage the hearer by moving from similar to different, from the familiar to the unfamiliar, as here, from our own interest in wisdom, seen in language, to that of the Hebrews.

In "Death" (the one sermon of these in the collection I heard live in 2007), the design is an imagined conversation with a deceased friend, a meditation on "The God of Untimely Death." Wildman confesses: "I instinctively reach for the Hebrew Bible's wisdom literature" when facing the endless train of death, the vagaries of "cavalier liberal brethren" and the inadequacy of Personalism:

> If I have to believe in God as a personal, aware, active creator, then I need an ancient worldview to match. I would gladly serve a God who creates the way Genesis hints, lovingly making each creature, fully formed, responsive to God's gift of life. If God has to be a big and powerful person, then give me Genesis or give me nothing! To hell with the countless death pits of our planetary history, to hell with the meandering experimentation of evolution, and to hell with coincidence and bad luck and pointless suffering and meaningless murder and being in the wrong place at the wrong time. In fact, to hell with untimely death. If God has to be a superperson who knows and cares and protects, then give me a world where evil acts of mass murder are never the outworking of mental illness and social torture but always simply the wicked deeds of bad people. Give me a God with a plan, even though I can't grasp its purpose. Give me Ecclesiastes!

Here Wildman reminds us of Edmund Steimle, of blessed memory, and particularly of sermons like his classic, "Address Not Known." Like Steimle, Wildman has in his sights "many theological liberals." For Wildman, again, God is best pictured as "the Ground of Being—the depth structures of nature and the wellsprings of value." Yet, we sense that his deceased friend (whose voice we do not hear in the sermon) might, we could imagine, respond thus to Wildman: "There is a kind of presence in God's absence. There is a power in personhood though God is before and beyond personality. There is ever the power and possibility of love though God has given us the 'freedom to go straight to hell if we so choose' (Tutu). There is mystery, aplenty, in all creation. There is creation, even though there is more and fuller evidence of fall. But there is also new creation, though the pains of the old creation are ever so evident."

Foreword

In fact, the careful design of the sermon not only invites, but also requires us, to some measure, to imagine what his dear, silent, deceased friend might have said. Or what we might say.

In "Creator," the design relies squarely on personal experience. The rhetorical form of the sermon is reflection upon personal experience, Wildman's experience as an "evangelical liberal." Note his irenic spirit, speaking of liberals and conservatives: "We do have a great deal in common, including our love of children, our celebration of our mothers and fathers, our preference for peaceful neighborhoods, our quest for health and happiness, and our conviction that life is best lived in relation to an ultimate reality that suffuses everyday events and transcends everyday concerns. But despite these shared life goals, mutual suspicion and hostility are very real." Reality, authority, history, church—all these split liberals from conservatives. And speaking of personal experience: "To Darwin, God gradually seemed less personal, benevolent, attentive, and active. Either God or evolution must go. That revelation demands not atheism—not for Darwin and not for us today either—but a different conception of the divine." This sermon, out of experience, rejects a personal, benevolent, attentive, active God—because of the evolutionary harshness of the process of creation. All preachers, younger and older, will do well to try to wrestle with the ways this preacher is himself wrestling with the traditions of Christian preaching, and its theological architectures and structures. At all events, these sermons give us the opportunity to meditate on their various designs, and so on sermon design in our own work.

A dear friend, a venerable and now superannuated preacher, the Rev. Gordon Knapp, one of the consistently best Methodist preachers of his era and area, recently wrote in an unpublished essay, "The Preaching Tree":

> Historically, there are Roman Catholic and Episcopalian priests, Lutheran pastors and Methodist preachers. However, the designation preacher does not sit well with many contemporary United Methodist clergy. Most prefer to be known as ministers or change agents or CEOs or pastoral counselors or religious enablers. With the popular connotation of the word "preach" being the presentation of boring, banal and unwanted advice, little wonder clergy dread to be known as preacher. Despite the negative image, preacher continues to remain an honorable designation, signifying someone who espouses and presents the Christian faith. Even with the plethora of today's electronic gimmickry, preaching continues to be the primary means by which Christianity is kept

before those who claim to profess it, those who wish to fine tune it, and those in need of hearing its demands and promises. The late William Barclay (that wonderful old Scotsman) suggested that four essential aspects of preaching are captured Greek in words: *kerygma, didiche, paraklesis* and *homilia*. To me, these terms suggest the analogy of a tree; a Preaching Tree with its roots, trunk, blossoms and fruit of the Gospel message.

Professor Wildman holds onto the designation, preacher, and preaches under the shading, luxurious branches of such a preaching tree.

In all, it is a happy, welcome moment to have the pleasure to welcome Professor Wildman's sermons, in print. Herein he does challenge us to know and speak the truth, or what truth we know to speak. Herein he does wrestle with the traditions within the Great Tradition, the various days within the great and lasting Day of God. Herein he does school us in the varieties of sermon design, of forms in rhetoric, many of which can themselves be used in other sermons, by different preachers in different voices (and, of course, novel content, with quotations and citations as necessary). Herein he does carry us into ranges of Holy Scripture, some familiar and some less, against the backdrop of seasonal and lectionary readings. Herein, with vigor, Wildman announces the Gospel of the God Who Is: "This God is the very Ground of Being, the depth structures and dynamic flows of life, the cosmic Dao and the God beyond God of our beloved mystics. This God waits for the unfolding of nature itself, of our very lives."

Preface

SERMONS MAY NEVER HOPE to capture the reality or the richness of God. A series of sermons may attempt to draw out balancing insights, but a single sermon must be one sided if its point is not to be lost in the concept-mocking richness and distinction-defying simplicity of the divine life. It follows that the preacher must resist the temptation to try to say everything, out of respect for the limitations of language and competence. Since my faith is fixed upon the God beyond God—that is, on the ultimate reality beyond all beings, including beyond all divine beings, indeed beyond all Being—I am particularly hard pressed by limitations of language and competence. This book represents an attempt to grapple with this profound challenge, without meekly (and probably wisely) surrendering to silence. In these sermons, fragment by fragment, angle by angle, I attempt kaleidoscopically to conjure the mystery of life, the purity of grace, the bliss of surrender, and the God beyond God. To me, this is the most profound part of Christianity and it resonates with profound insights of other wisdom traditions.

The season of my homiletical journey covered in these sermons began in September 1993 when I transitioned from parish ministry into the very different world of seminary teaching. In my first month of teaching at Boston University's School of Theology, I accepted an invitation to preach at the seminary's service of worship in Marsh Chapel. I announced my radical mystical theology with a sermon titled "God Is . . . Holy Mystery." A year later—with preaching having become an uncommon adventure—I preached on the flip side of that coin with "God Is . . . Friend." From that time for several years, I occasionally preached on facets of divine reality, beginning the title of each sermon with "God is . . ."—thus the title of this book.

Many of these sermons were difficult and demanding for hearers. I abandoned my long-standing pattern of using concrete illustrations, exegeses of Scripture readings, a smattering of funny stories, "Peanuts" cartoons, and feel-good one liners, which help to lighten the burden of listening. Instead of my usual extemporizing, I followed a text to optimize control over my language. Instead of moving around and engaging my listeners, I stayed fixed in the pulpit and limited movement to hands and face. I showed no mercy to my listeners! Those present were sometimes faced with strange theological reflection and mysterious poetic images. But they always had a text available for consulting afterwards.

These are not sermons for beginners in the journey of faith, nor sermons I could have preached in the churches to which I have ministered. They were sermons for a place dedicated to striving after intellectual and spiritual maturity, or at least poor excuses for such sermons. As my friend and former colleague Tony Campbell said of one of them, "It would not fly outside these walls, brother . . . but it did fly in here."

We should be thankful that there are pulpits where we can strive after expression of our deepest and hardest thoughts about ultimate reality; places where each of us can preach to one another, unencumbered by the all-too-real constraints of much parish preaching; places where we can bring our longing for understanding and wholeness and lay it unabashedly upon the altar.

Marsh Chapel's preachers and Boston University School of Theology's community of worshippers has been that for me. I treasure that distinctive pulpit, with its harsh delights and never-ending stream of odd-ball occupants. I urge seminary students to treasure it also. They should treasure it while they can, for when in due course they leave the seminary haven for the joys and frustrations of preaching and listening to sermons in churches, they will remember, perhaps with ambivalent amazement, that many of the sermons preached in their seminary would not fly outside its walls, whether because they were difficult or bad or both—and maybe they will even long to be in such an adventurous place once again.

The Sermons

All readings are from the New Revised Standard Version of the Bible.

God Is . . . Holy Mystery
Marsh Chapel, Boston University, Seminary Worship Service,
 September 30, 1993
Readings: Job 8:20–9:20; Revelation 19:11–21
Text: "He would crush me with a storm" (Job 8:17a)

God Is . . . Friend
Marsh Chapel, Boston University, Seminary Worship Service,
 October 20, 1994
Readings: Isaiah 52:13–53:12; Psalm 35; Mark 10:35–45
Text: "I went about mourning as though for my friend" (Psalms 35:14a)

God Is . . . Hope
Marsh Chapel, Boston University, Seminary Worship Service,
 February 1, 1996
Readings: Isaiah 51:1–11; Romans 8:18–25
Text: "And sorrow and sighing will flee away" (Isaiah 51:11e)

God Is . . . Monarch
Marsh Chapel, Boston University, Seminary Alumni Reunion Service,
 May 17, 1997
Reading: 1 Samuel 8:1–22
Text: "Appoint for us, then, a king to govern us, like other nations"
 (1 Samuel 8:5b)

The Sermons

God Is . . . Wisdom
Marsh Chapel, Boston University, Seminary Worship Service, September 9, 1997
Readings: Psalm 19; Proverbs 1:20–33; James 3:1; Mark 8:31–36
Text: "You are setting your mind not on divine things but on human things" (Mark 8:33b)

God Is . . . Coming
Marsh Chapel, Boston University, University Worship Service, November 27, 2005
Scripture: Isaiah 64:1–9; Mark 13:24–37
Text: "O that you would tear open the heavens and come down" (Isaiah 64:1a)

God Is . . . Death
Marsh Chapel, Boston University, Seminary Worship Service, April 25, 2007
Scriptures: Ecclesiastes 3
Text: "A time to die" (Ecclesiastes 3:2)

God Is . . . Creator (aka Narnia's Aslan, Earth's Darwin, and Heaven's God)
Marsh Chapel, Boston University, Boston University Worship Service, June 21, 2009
Readings: Psalm 8; Job 38:1–7; John 1:1–5
Text: "Where were you when I laid the foundation of the earth?" (Job 38:4a)

God Is . . . Waiting
Marsh Chapel, Boston University, Seminary Worship Service, December 10, 2014
Readings: Isaiah 40:1–11; Psalm 85:1–2, 8–13; 2 Peter 3:8–15a; Mark 1:1–8
Text: "Therefore, beloved, while you are waiting for these things" (2 Peter 3:14)

A Prayer before Each Sermon

(written by Rev. Dr. Andrew Dutney)

[silently]
Lord Jesus Christ,
Although my words will undoubtedly humiliate you,
Please accept them all the same;
And through the humiliation of preaching
May we be encountered by you
Who bore the humiliation of incarnation
And the cross
For our sake and the world's.

[spoken]
In the name of the Father,
and of the Son,
and of the Holy Spirit.

God Is . . . Holy Mystery

READINGS

[Job's friend said:]
See, God will not reject a blameless person, nor take the hand of evildoers.
He will yet fill your mouth with laughter, and your lips with shouts of joy.
Those who hate you will be clothed with shame, and the tent of the wicked will be no more.
Then Job answered:
Indeed I know that this is so; but how can a mortal be just before God?
If one wished to contend with him, one could not answer him once in a thousand.
He is wise in heart, and mighty in strength—who has resisted him, and succeeded?—
he who removes mountains, and they do not know it, when he overturns them in his anger;
who shakes the earth out of its place, and its pillars tremble;
who commands the sun, and it does not rise; who seals up the stars;
who alone stretched out the heavens and trampled the waves of the Sea;
who made the Bear and Orion, the Pleiades and the chambers of the south;
who does great things beyond understanding, and marvellous things without number.
Look, he passes by me, and I do not see him; he moves on, but I do not perceive him.

God Is . . .

He snatches away; who can stop him? Who will say to him, "What are you doing?"

God will not turn back his anger; the helpers of Rahab bowed beneath him.

How then can I answer him, choosing my words with him?

Though I am innocent, I cannot answer him; I must appeal for mercy to my accuser.

If I summoned him and he answered me, I do not believe that he would listen to my voice.

For he crushes me with a tempest, and multiplies my wounds without cause;

he will not let me get my breath, but fills me with bitterness.

If it is a contest of strength, he is the strong one!

If it is a matter of justice, who can summon him?

Though I am innocent, my own mouth would condemn me;

though I am blameless, he would prove me perverse.

    JOB 8:20—9:20

Then I saw heaven opened, and there was a white horse! Its rider is called Faithful and True, and in righteousness he judges and makes war. His eyes are like a flame of fire, and on his head are many diadems; and he has a name inscribed that no one knows but himself. He is clothed in a robe dipped in blood, and his name is called The Word of God. And the armies of heaven, wearing fine linen, white and pure, were following him on white horses. From his mouth comes a sharp sword with which to strike down the nations, and he will rule them with a rod of iron; he will tread the wine press of the fury of the wrath of God the Almighty. On his robe and on his thigh he has a name inscribed, "King of kings and Lord of lords."

Then I saw an angel standing in the sun, and with a loud voice he called to all the birds that fly in mid-heaven, "Come, gather for the great supper of God, to eat the flesh of kings, the flesh of captains, the flesh of the mighty, the flesh of horses and their riders—flesh of all, both free and slave, both small and great." Then I saw the beast and the kings of the earth with their armies gathered to make war against the rider on the horse and against his army. And the beast was captured, and with it the false prophet who had performed in its presence the signs by which he deceived those who had received the mark of the beast and those who worshipped its image. These two were thrown alive into the lake of fire that burns with sulphur. And the rest were killed by the sword of the rider on the horse, the sword that came from his mouth; and all the birds were gorged with their flesh.

REVELATION 19:11–21

MEDITATION

We always do well to reflect on our place before God and our conduct toward each other. When we consider that God is Love, we understand that we should love God with all our heart, soul, mind and strength, and love our neighbor as ourselves. When we ponder God as Goodness, we know we should strive for excellence in character and faithfulness of witness. When we meditate on God as Creator, we should rejoice in the wonder of life, even as life's ambiguity leads us to strengthen our determination to create new life with each step that we take in the world. What, then, should we be and do in light of the fact that God is Holy Mystery?

God is holiness, surely, means that we should recognize the majesty of God in sacred praise and holy obedience; we should know that God does not look lightly upon the injustice and cruelty of our human societies; we should sense ourselves called to realize the divine kingdom and do the divine will on earth and in our lives. God is mystery, surely, means that we should trust the divine will even when we cannot understand its purpose. It means that the words and images we use to praise God and reflect on the divine nature will always be inadequate to their object, so that we must approach worship and theology alike in humility, always ready to discover further reaches of the unfathomable richness of divine life.

We might even consider that, in a culture obsessed with personal self-improvement on the one hand, and material wealth on the other, a heightened awareness of God as holy mystery might not go astray. It could go a long way toward checking some of the absurdities of contemporary life, such as new age yuppies wearing specially shaped crystals to enhance their harmony with the earth at the same time as carrying on protracted, vituperous arguments with neighbors about the placement of new outdoor decks and swimming pools and rooflines. It might also make us more realistic about the abysmal conditions of life for most people on our planet, more cautious about plunging headlong into the environmental unknown, more hesitant to claim understanding of everything we try to control, from genes and atoms to societies and economies. God as Holy Mystery may be a message tailor made for our situation.

You can see how this line of thought would unfold. There would be an essentially moral message about how properly appreciating the holy mystery of God leads us to reappraise our lives and our societies in a truly radical way. Fine. I think there is nothing wrong with any of that. But it seems faintly diluted, perhaps a little trivial, and certainly over-confident. I think the passages from Job and Revelation take us in another direction. God is Holy Mystery, yes, but in a profound, unsettling, even terrifying way.

How grateful we should be that there is preserved in the Hebrew Bible this insight of Jewish wisdom literature: "For he crushes me with a tempest, and multiplies my wounds without cause; he will not let me get my breath, but fills me with bitterness." The Christian tradition is dominated by the themes of sin and salvation, by biblical images of God as Creator and Father, Mother and Lover, Redeemer and Friend. It is jarring, then, to encounter Job's description of God as overwhelmingly awesome, as crushingly powerful, as violent and capricious, as unaccountable to any moral standards: "If it is a contest of strength, he is the strong one! If it is a matter of justice, who can summon him?" Job's innocence and righteousness offer him no protection from the divine fierceness. Nor is there any refuge for us from the destroyer. We are prone, naked, exposed, endangered, helpless, and hopeless in the divine presence. There is no higher court to which we can take our complaint about God's merciless power. There being no recourse, then, we must suffer and be crushed with no consolation; nothing can protect us.

We might enlarge upon the divine destructiveness by considering that about us which is destroyed. Indeed, we might try to excuse God with clever distinctions. Our evil natures, our pride, and our sloth are destroyed, we might say, but our redeemed natures are increased. Our self-assurance and willfulness are smashed, we might speculate, but our responsible and mature instincts are strengthened. If there is truth in these distinctions, it is a premature truth. The deeper truth is that we are completely, utterly, exhaustively annihilated by the Holy Mystery that is God. Any sense of ourselves is lost in the divine presence. We exchange our joy and sadness for desolation beyond language, our pride and goodness for inconceivable emptiness, our concepts and desires for tears of hopelessness. Nothing of ourselves survives the encounter with the divine destroyer: "Come, gather for the great supper of God, to eat the flesh of kings, the flesh of captains, the flesh of the mighty, the flesh of horses and their riders—flesh of all, both free and slave, both small and great."

How we trivialize the divine Holy Mystery! We manage and control it, with an even greater degree of ignorance than plagues our dealings with each other and with our world. We hide from it with every ounce of energy we possess, as we deny our common humanity, our biological rootedness, our death. We even dare speak of the Holy Mystery in a measured way, systematically purging it of offense, morally purifying the divine character lest it be besmirched by our complaint against its capriciousness. In so doing we dance with ignorant anxiousness amongst the teeth of the dragon; we dance and sing together for illusory comfort. There is no comfort to be had. There is no escape. If God be immoral, if God hate us, or what is worse, if God be indifferent to our struggling for the very breath of life under the crushing weight of the storm, then what is to be done? As Job suggests, to whom may we appeal? The Holy Mystery transcends every moral category, and is a law unto itself. While ever we fail to grasp the dismaying possibility of divine neutrality and indifference to our pain, to our sense of outrage at life, to our ravaged societies, to our traumatized planet, we also fail to appreciate in even the most basic way the terror of the divine presence. There is no knowing with God. All of our wisdom, all of the assurance of salvation in Christ, all of the trusting in the divine benevolence—all of these are of no avail when God "fills me with bitterness" and "multiplies my wounds without cause." At that moment, every expectation is shattered, every pattern broken, every security irrelevant. We are at the mercy of God as the bear with its claw to our throats.

It is no wonder, then, that atheistic objections to God can have some moral momentum; that the histories of paganism and of sadism and masochism have religious aspects; that the mana of the shaman in tribal religions is respected despite its amoral, capricious quality; that women who are especially submissive have been worshipped in our culturally confused way as especially pure and holy; and that religion is rightly regarded as a protective haven, not from the world, but from God.

God Is . . .

We may not recognize God as our refuge, "our ever-present help in time of trouble," until we have first understood in the depths of our being that we have no refuge from the divine terror. For it is only in the moment of surrender, in the immediate proximity of death, under the claw of the bear, that the proper relation between us creatures and God is fully realized. God may indeed crush us to death, or rip us apart, but we are God's creatures even as this happens.

How easily do we presume upon the divine grace! How brazenly we approach the civilized courts of Holy Majesty to lay our case before a manageable God, tamed by divine promises of salvation. How cavalierly we dismiss the divine wildness, as if love were not wild and dangerous, as if grace were not every bit as much fiendish foe as familiar friend. We have no rights before God and no claim upon the divine compassion. Again, deliverance cannot be understood even faintly until we realize how proper it is that we should relinquish even our divinely assured claims to it.

So how is it that the Holy Mystery is cognizant of us, mindful of our lives, tolerant of our attempts to love, even loving us in our confusion? How indeed. To answer that this divine interest has been revealed, or that it is evident in the effusive glory of nature, is often to retreat from the mystery once again, to seek refuge in assurance of the divine love when there is finally no such assurance. It is prematurely to batten down the hatches when what is required is the stinging salt air. Michael Leunig, an Australian poet and artist, puts it well:

> When the heart
> Is cut or cracked or broken,
> Do not clutch it
> Let the wound lie open
> Let the wind
> From the good old sea blow in
> To bathe the wound with salt
> And let it sting
> Let a stray dog lick it
> Let a bird lean in the hole and sing
> A simple song like a tiny bell
> And let it ring

In this state of surrender, deliverance may or may not occur. When it happens, it is entirely at the instigation of God. This is the meaning of salvation by grace. Too often our interpretation of salvation by faith corresponds to an incursion on the divine freedom. While trusting the divine promises has its place, it must be founded on the awareness that we may not presume upon anything in the presence of Holy Mystery; not even what we take to be the divine promises. The supposed necessity of some atoning sacrifice to justify the divine decision to forgive can likewise be pressed into service as a way of controlling the freedom of Holy Mystery. What we learn from Job is that the Holy Mystery will not be controlled, not by nations or governments, nor by revelations or theologies, nor by worship, or praise, or promises, or faith, or hope, or love. And yet, we are not always crushed, and deliverance does find us. This inexplicable act of capricious love—of free divine grace—is the miracle upon which our continued survival depends every minute of every day.

It is no accident that the Hindu deity Śiva, the God of destruction, is so often pictured dancing. Nor is it coincidental that the Hindu conception of the divine action in history is sometimes characterized as līla, or "play." For joy is premised on peril. One can dance amongst the brutal teeth of the dragon in ignorance, or with the wise awareness of how great the danger is. Only in the latter case will the anxiety of the dancing and singing give way to ecstatic joy, which is delight.

We delight in God because God is Holy Mystery. We have no protection from the divine wildness, so we need have no inhibitions. There is no higher court of appeal with which we might attempt to tame the divine capriciousness, so we celebrate in our naked surrender. We are not obsessed with absurdly constructing ourselves like so many Lego blocks before the divine throne, so we are free to dance with the angels, those crazy unknown dancers whose innocence was never weighed down by the load of our existence.

We can sing, too. We can sing out the clumsy words of our liturgies, the fractured concepts of our theologies, because we know how inadequate they are to the Holy Mystery they seek to express. Those who take their prayers too seriously, or the contents of their own belabored minds too literally, risk being turgid grumps in the presence of irrepressible divine joy. To be sure, we need to use our language about God with the utmost care, but the first step in being responsible is to recognize that we are negotiating with Holy Mystery, and that our ideas of God are but an unstable, makeshift lattice above a vast chasm. The recognition of the inadequacy of our theological language is the first step toward intellectual responsibility. Delight is one of the most serious emotions we creatures can experience, because it is premised on the true awareness of the pointlessness of resisting or cooperating or negotiating with the divine terror.

And then to see this God, this Holy Mystery, come down from the lofty throne, to dance among us as a child, first alone as if unsure, and then holding hands and whooping up a joyful hullabaloo under the stars, dancing through our history, destroying and transforming. . . . To see this same one riding on a white horse, with eyes like blazing fire, dressed in a robe dipped in blood, armed with a sharp sword coming out of his mouth with which to strike down the nations. . . . To see this is wonder and awe, love and transforming power. We fear this one, even as we love, recoil in horror even as we are fascinated.

We forget the divine Holy Mystery at our peril. Our broken world dances anxiously amongst the teeth of the dragon, its future unknown. Too often the church sings its dreary songs there, too, having forgotten that the divine is too expansive even for the gospel to capture, foolishly infatuated with the comforting assurance of salvation. To learn to dance with honest terror, with simple wisdom, with disarming delight—this is to live. And what is more important—and profoundly, joyously pointless—this is how we show our love to the Holy Mysterious One in whose terrifying, tender hand we are held.

God Is . . . Friend

READINGS

See, my servant shall prosper;
   he shall be exalted and lifted up,
   and shall be very high.
Just as there were many who were astonished at him
    —so marred was his appearance, beyond human semblance,
   and his form beyond that of mortals—
so he shall startle many nations;
   kings shall shut their mouths because of him;
for that which had not been told them they shall see,
   and that which they had not heard they shall contemplate.
Who has believed what we have heard?
   And to whom has the arm of the Lord been revealed?
For he grew up before him like a young plant,
   and like a root out of dry ground;
he had no form or majesty that we should look at him,
   nothing in his appearance that we should desire him.
He was despised and rejected by others;
   a man of suffering and acquainted with infirmity;
and as one from whom others hide their faces
   he was despised, and we held him of no account.
Surely he has borne our infirmities
   and carried our diseases;
yet we accounted him stricken,

struck down by God, and afflicted.
But he was wounded for our transgressions,
   crushed for our iniquities;
upon him was the punishment that made us whole,
   and by his bruises we are healed.
All we like sheep have gone astray;
   we have all turned to our own way,
and the Lord has laid on him
   the iniquity of us all.
He was oppressed, and he was afflicted,
   yet he did not open his mouth;
like a lamb that is led to the slaughter,
   and like a sheep that before its shearers is silent,
   so he did not open his mouth.
By a perversion of justice he was taken away.
   Who could have imagined his future?
For he was cut off from the land of the living,
   stricken for the transgression of my people.
They made his grave with the wicked
   and his tomb with the rich,
although he had done no violence,
   and there was no deceit in his mouth.
Yet it was the will of the Lord to crush him with pain.
When you make his life an offering for sin,
   he shall see his offspring, and shall prolong his days;
through him the will of the Lord shall prosper.
   Out of his anguish he shall see light;
he shall find satisfaction through his knowledge.
   The righteous one, my servant, shall make many righteous,
   and he shall bear their iniquities.
Therefore I will allot him a portion with the great,
   and he shall divide the spoil with the strong;
because he poured out himself to death,
   and was numbered with the transgressors;
yet he bore the sin of many,
   and made intercession for the transgressors.

     Isaiah 52:13–53:12

God Is . . . Friend

Contend, O Lord, with those who contend with me;
   fight against those who fight against me!
Take hold of shield and buckler,
   and rise up to help me!
Draw the spear and javelin
   against my pursuers;
say to my soul,
   "I am your salvation."
Let them be put to shame and dishonour
   who seek after my life.
Let them be turned back and confounded
   who devise evil against me.
Let them be like chaff before the wind,
   with the angel of the Lord driving them on.
Let their way be dark and slippery,
   with the angel of the Lord pursuing them.
For without cause they hid their net for me;
   without cause they dug a pit for my life.
Let ruin come on them unawares.
And let the net that they hid ensnare them;
   let them fall in it—to their ruin.
Then my soul shall rejoice in the Lord,
   exulting in his deliverance.
All my bones shall say,
   " O Lord, who is like you?
You deliver the weak
   from those too strong for them,
   the weak and needy from those who despoil them."
Malicious witnesses rise up;
   they ask me about things I do not know.
They repay me evil for good;
   my soul is forlorn.
But as for me, when they were sick,
   I wore sackcloth;
   I afflicted myself with fasting.

God Is . . .

I prayed with head bowed on my bosom,
   as though I grieved for a friend or a brother;
I went about as one who laments for a mother,
   bowed down and in mourning.
But at my stumbling they gathered in glee,
   they gathered together against me;
ruffians whom I did not know
   tore at me without ceasing;
they impiously mocked more and more,
   gnashing at me with their teeth.
How long, O Lord, will you look on?
   Rescue me from their ravages,
   my life from the lions!
Then I will thank you in the great congregation;
   in the mighty throng I will praise you.
Do not let my treacherous enemies rejoice over me,
   or those who hate me without cause wink the eye.
For they do not speak peace,
   but they conceive deceitful words
   against those who are quiet in the land.
They open wide their mouths against me;
   they say, "Aha, Aha,
   our eyes have seen it."
You have seen, O Lord; do not be silent!
   O Lord, do not be far from me!
Wake up! Bestir yourself for my defence,
   for my cause, my God and my Lord!
Vindicate me, O Lord, my God,
   according to your righteousness,
   and do not let them rejoice over me.
Do not let them say to themselves,
   "Aha, we have our heart's desire."
Do not let them say, "We have swallowed you up."
Let all those who rejoice at my calamity
   be put to shame and confusion;
let those who exalt themselves against me

be clothed with shame and dishonour.
Let those who desire my vindication
 shout for joy and be glad,
 and say evermore,
"Great is the LORD,
 who delights in the welfare of his servant."
Then my tongue shall tell of your righteousness
 and of your praise all day long.
  PSALM 35

James and John, the sons of Zebedee, came forward to him and said to him, "Teacher, we want you to do for us whatever we ask of you." And he said to them, "What is it you want me to do for you?" And they said to him, "Grant us to sit, one at your right hand and one at your left, in your glory." But Jesus said to them, "You do not know what you are asking. Are you able to drink the cup that I drink, or be baptized with the baptism that I am baptized with?" They replied, "We are able." Then Jesus said to them, "The cup that I drink you will drink; and with the baptism with which I am baptized, you will be baptized; but to sit at my right hand or at my left is not mine to grant, but it is for those for whom it has been prepared."

When the ten heard this, they began to be angry with James and John. So Jesus called them and said to them, "You know that among the Gentiles those whom they recognize as their rulers lord it over them, and their great ones are tyrants over them. But it is not so among you; but whoever wishes to become great among you must be your servant, and whoever wishes to be first among you must be slave of all. For the Son of Man came not to be served but to serve, and to give his life a ransom for many."

  MARK 10:35–45

MEDITATION

To speak of God as "friend" is, unavoidably, to use a broken symbol, to speak in a way that is simultaneously fitting and misleading. To pursue the question of fit and distortion, we might ask how it could be that God is friend. There are plenty of theological-metaphysical answers to this question but they are better suited to a theology class, so I shall set those aside for now.

Instead, let's bypass the question of how it can be that we rightly call God "friend" and speak instead of the meaning-for-us of this affirmation.

In Mark's story about James and John approaching Jesus for a special favor, it turns out that they want a special place in Jesus' kingdom, in accordance with what they thought was the exceptional level of their commitment and enthusiasm. There is something childish about this request. It is like students sidling up to their teacher in the middle of the semester and asking for an A+ on the class—before they had even made a presentation, composed a paper, or taken a test.

It appears, therefore, that we can fault the James and John of the story for not really appreciating the seriousness of their request, and perhaps also for their insensitivity in placing a triumphal reading on Jesus' slow journey to Jerusalem, which for Mark's Jesus is a tense, terse drive toward a clearly anticipated fate. But does Mark's Jesus fault James and John for their audacity? No. Far from it, in fact. Jesus, not without a textual smile, tolerates the enthusiasm of his beloved disciples, and even transforms their fumbling after spiritual greatness with his suddenly shared insight that their ambition will in a sense be realized, for they will drink from the cup that Jesus drinks, and be baptized with his baptism.

But isn't Jesus supposed to get angry at their juvenile enthusiasm and their insensitivity to the ways of the kingdom of God? And doesn't Jesus do just this in the story? Well, actually no. The pericope presents Jesus having a heart-felt conversation with James and John, and leading them deeper into their own love and service of God. Jesus is only prompted to a blunter form of education when the ten start expressing their irritation. And what does he say then? Mark has Jesus address the disciples' jealousy, which is probably a reference to a live problem in the author's faith community. To be sure, with his remarks about the greatest being the servant of all, Jesus indirectly continues his conversation with James and John. But he is primarily concerned with chastising the ten for their envious anger at James and John, and most likely their irritation with Jesus himself for not brushing off the enthusiastic youngsters.

So what are we to make of this story? Just this: Jesus does not liken James and John to the competitive Gentiles for approaching him with their youthful love and ambition; on the contrary, he deepens the two brothers in their enthusiasm, steadies them, and shows them what their longing for spiritual greatness really means. The brothers approach Jesus as their friend, entrusting him with their dreams and ambition, and Jesus acts like their friend, wisely and surely leading them deeper into their own love for God. Who else but a friend would hear such ill-formed ambition? To whom but a friend would we dare risk the sharing of such longings? Mark's memory of the friendship between Jesus, James, and John is a parable of divine friendship. God's friendship is like the active concern Jesus displays for his friends: God is a conversation partner, a sounding board, a wise listener, a caring educator of souls.

This is without doubt one of the most scandalous aspects of the Christian gospel. How could we ever feel justified, let alone comfortable, speaking and acting as a friend of the holy mysterious One, the abysmal Ground of Being, the one that undoes us with a glance, before whom the nations shrink and the universe itself trembles? How indeed? Nevertheless, the Christian gospel declares the friendship of God with confidence grounded in its encounter with Jesus Christ, in whom the hospitality of reality disclosed itself with stunning concreteness.

Have you ever wondered why Christian worship often drops out parts of some of the Psalms, focusing instead on the more uplifting bits? The Psalms that get treated in this way tend to be full of aggressive imagery, in which, say, David gives vent to his almost uncontrollable desire for all kinds of horrors to be visited upon his enemies. In fact, in such Psalms David is usually found begging God to do these horrible things, thereby to prove the divine love, to show that God knows which end of the rod of justice to hold. And what does God stand to gain from this deal? If God acts in the way that David believes is just and right, then David will praise God in public, making a big fuss over the fact that God took his side. These are what I call the "Get-'em-for-me-God" Psalms. Psalm 35 belongs squarely in this category.

It is not so easy to explain this I'll-scratch-your-back-if-you'll-scratch-mine type of prayerful negotiation to Christian congregations who are usually encouraged to reject bargaining with God as irrelevant at best and blasphemous at worst. Nor is it easy to give an uplifting account of David's poisonous desire for revenge to people who are rightly taught from an early age to suppress the feelings of rage and violation to which David gives colorful expression.

Perhaps it is not so difficult to see, then, why Christians are in the habit of editing the "Get-'em-for-me-God" Psalms. And why not edit? "Saul has killed his thousands; David his ten-thousands." Surely we are dealing in these Psalms with the megalomaniacal side of David, and his blood-lust for revenge and violence to which he often gave numerically impressive expression. This man badly needs to listen to the Sermon on the Mount, we might say; perhaps he should be locked up, or perhaps his country ought to be invaded to deliver his people from the devastating scourge of his rule. And as for the Hebrew Scripture's interpretation of David's horrendous problems with his kids as punishment for his dastardly behavior in the Bathsheba and Uriah incident, that is clearly post-facto rationalization—it is not surprising that kids turn hostile with a father like that.

It is true that these Psalms enhance our insight into a fascinating, unusual figure of history, one whose exploits are not just anyone's cup of tea. And it is very likely that the personal spirituality of such a larger-than-life figure might not be the best model for our own or our children's spiritual formation. But—all this said—we edit the "Get-'em-for-me-God" Psalms at our peril. These Psalms capture the realism of human political and social life, they recall to our immunized minds that very little in human affairs is accomplished without the use of power, they vividly capture the timeless truth that the exercise of political and military power leaves no one lily-white pure with unvarnished motivations, they are stark reminders of the eviscerating pain of victimization and betrayal, and they relentlessly press the claim of revenge for legitimacy.

Above all, the "Get-'em-for-me-God" Psalms offer hope that God is relevant to life with these dimensions, to boisterous, blistering, boundlessly normal life. And relevant how? Not as Supreme Judge, because David, and we with him, suffer at the hands of divine judgment every bit as much as those whose mercilessness he and we decry. Not as Benevolent Monarch, for we appear to a significant extent to be stuck with the job of running the sociopolitical show ourselves. Not as Wise Creator, for the wisdom of creation so ordered is unsurpassably difficult to discern. Not as Loving Parent, for God's warring children are undone and the workings of divine love are obscured in our comprehensive self-destructiveness. Not as Holy Mystery, for there is neither retribution nor justice but only despair and inexplicable delight in that direction. How then is God relevant to our world of wistful longings, of wrenching agonies, of wild violence, of wickedness and wretchedness and wars and want and waste?

God Is . . . Friend

God counts in this, our world, as friend and advocate. God as friend means that God takes our side in a dispute. God as friend means that God sees our lives from our point of view. God as friend means that God can be expected to act on our behalf. God as friend means that God can be cajoled, pressured, manipulated, bribed, flattered—or at least, we can count on God to tolerate our attempts to twist the divine holiness around our little fingers in these ways. Who but a powerful friend and advocate is useful in the face of the dehumanizing, enraging, deathly anonymity of those who at this very moment are being systematically starved, at this very moment brutally raped, at this very moment mercilessly tortured, at this very moment simply—oh so simply—hacked or shot or hung or knifed or beat to their senseless, pointless, premature deaths? Who but a friend would see and care and moan and cry and be bewildered and enraged and disoriented, and half-consciously, deliriously scream for equally merciless, relentlessly brutal revenge on behalf of the silenced one? Who but a fine friend could bear to be beside us as the ravages of the human condition are poured out bloodlike onto the barren earth as a useless offering for no discernible benefit? Who but a divine friend could bear to see human souls treated with such chilling heartlessness, such careless depravity? Who but a merciful and holy friend could be entrusted with the overwhelming, mute sadness that envelops us when we realize our condition, our pitiful, hapless condition, our self-inflicted, self-defeating, stupid, senseless, serenely ignorant condition? To whom but a wise and patient friend could we entrust our longing to destroy the destroyers, to vent our rage upon the merciless, to rip ourselves to pieces out of sorrow and remorse, to dive into the abyss of comforting, self-annihilating nothingness when for a moment we see how shattered and desperate we have become since we were innocent infants, when we see for a moment the price of self-conscious freedom in the world.

God, Friend, save us from our fury! God, Friend, save us from our cruel sanction of cruelty, our thoughtless participation in perpetual violence! God, Friend, save us from each other! "You have seen, O LORD; do not be silent! O Lord, do not be far from me! Wake up! Bestir yourself for my defence, for my cause, my God and my Lord!"

And what of the suffering innocents, the tortured, the slain, the beaten—the silent forgotten ones who haunt our hearts, struggling for a memorial in the busy freedom of our lives? They themselves uttered David's words—even the hateful among them—with a desperation not even David knew: "Let them be put to shame and dishonour who seek after my life. Let them be turned back and confounded who devise evil against me. Let them be like chaff before the wind, with the angel of the Lord driving them on. Let their way be dark and slippery, with the angel of the Lord pursuing them. . . . How long, O Lord, will you look on? Rescue me from their ravages, my life from the lions!"

Oh, they would surely praise God were their deliverance to materialize. But as the trigger pulls loudly, as the rope snaps taut, as the knife flashes fast, as the starved body yields to blank staring, as the nails are hammered hard home, David's words are rekindled on their grimacing lips: "How long, O Lord, will you look on?" They walk the earth, Jesus among them, mourning their friend, their God-Friend, their absent, impotent God-Friend to whom they cried in vain, their broken-down God-Friend scattered into the souls of millions as hope betrayed; they tread the grey plains unmemorialized, uncomforted by the hope of a distant, irrelevant resurrection of their punished bodies, earth to anonymous earth, ashes to empty ashes, dust to blinding, stinging dust.

Can the suffering of this host of souls be redeemed? Can it be returned to human societies as living justice, as transformative power, as justified hope? Or must it remain darkly buried in the swollen belly of history, the trampled playground of the great human moral kindergarten, an ignored trophy to human progress? It is a pitiful falsehood to say that suffering ennobles the human soul, as fire hardens and purifies precious metal. The truth is that suffering mostly crushes: it wears down its victims, until they hide it away for fear that all will be lost to its blunt claim; or it does its work of destruction so completely that no one remembers.

Isaiah seems aware of this when he refrains from trivializing the suffering of the servant by pretending that its offensiveness can somehow be purged. Rather, Isaiah reaches deep into the imaginative heart of his tradition, the tradition of a community that memorializes suffering, and discerns with stunning clarity that, though suffering remains an offense, and cannot be redeemed in itself, it can sometimes redeem. "He was despised and rejected by others; a man of suffering and acquainted with infirmity; and as one from whom others hide their faces he was despised, and we held him of no account. Surely he has borne our infirmities and carried our diseases; yet we accounted him stricken, struck down by God, and afflicted. But he was wounded for our transgressions, crushed for our iniquities; upon him was the punishment that made us whole, and by his bruises we are healed." Suffering, when memorialized within a community, can sometimes redeem. Isaiah's hope is ours, for we too memorialize suffering at the heart of our faith, and our history testifies to its redemptive power.

Yet, while this redemption is genuinely effective in our history, the hard facts remain that the sufferings of many are remembered by no one but God, and that many cries to this God-Friend for deliverance echo in the cavernous sky, searching in vain for an advocate who will end the pain, and rout those who inflict it. Our God-Friend is fickle, it seems. Is it for nothing that we entrust our cries for justice, for revenge, for very life, to this divine friend? We want not merely to be protected from our vengeful, murderous hearts, but for God to avenge us, and to avenge the silent, heart-stopped walkers who know their way on the ravaged face of the earth from the familiarity of endlessly retracing their pale steps. We want what David wanted: for God to get them for us. God's patience, God's silence, God's absence, is inexplicable, alarming, enraging. Must the advocacy of this friend then be decried after all as advocacy merely of the powerful, as undiscerning confirmation of those who dominate, as sham and shame? Must we judge God's friendship to be not only fickle, but farcical?

Yes we must. The point of Psalm 35 is that we must condemn our friend, we must complain and bitterly protest, for we can be friends in no other way. To edit our rage, to hide our disappointment, is to transform this friend into a dangerous, unknown stranger, and no lover of our souls. So we must rage, and cry, and beat our breast, and fall on our faces—for this and only this is to be friend to our divine Friend. We edit the Psalm at our peril, for it is to edit our very hearts, it is to cease trusting our friend, it is to surrender to evil in the world, it is to exchange the hope of companionship for the cold embrace of lonely wandering. It would be as if James and John never approached Jesus with their hearts in their hands, longing for a companion who would not belittle their fiery ambition, who could sense their anxious yearning. It would be as if they turned aside, looking wistfully, from across a great chasm, at the distant stranger, never to be friend—and then left with their lonely, longing, and now grieving hearts.

From so far away they could never recognize their God-Friend dying in the death of this stranger, never feel the hope of the redemption of savage suffering, never be ennobled and emboldened by divine friendship to trust the God-Friend with the blunt honesty of their souls.

Editing our hearts is the great betrayal of divine friendship. It is to make divine friendship a half-truth, that neither-here-nor-there beast that sings the spirit into deadly slumber. If God is friend, then we must take this broken symbol seriously. We must join David and Isaiah and James and John in speaking our hearts to God, in entrusting to God our juvenile ambitions, our dark desires, our confusion and fury, our longings and fears, and our clumsy expressions of love. Friendship will brook nothing less.

God Is ... Hope

READINGS

Listen to me, you that pursue righteousness,
    you that seek the Lord.
Look to the rock from which you were hewn,
    and to the quarry from which you were dug.
Look to Abraham your father
    and to Sarah who bore you;
for he was but one when I called him,
    but I blessed him and made him many.
For the Lord will comfort Zion;
    he will comfort all her waste places,
and will make her wilderness like Eden,
    her desert like the garden of the Lord;
joy and gladness will be found in her,
    thanksgiving and the voice of song.
Listen to me, my people,
    and give heed to me, my nation;
for a teaching will go out from me,
    and my justice for a light to the peoples.
I will bring near my deliverance swiftly,
    my salvation has gone out
    and my arms will rule the peoples;
the coastlands wait for me,
    and for my arm they hope.

God Is . . .

Lift up your eyes to the heavens,
  and look at the earth beneath;
for the heavens will vanish like smoke,
  the earth will wear out like a garment,
  and those who live on it will die like gnats;
but my salvation will be for ever,
  and my deliverance will never be ended.
Listen to me, you who know righteousness,
  you people who have my teaching in your hearts;
do not fear the reproach of others,
  and do not be dismayed when they revile you.
For the moth will eat them up like a garment,
  and the worm will eat them like wool;
but my deliverance will be for ever,
  and my salvation to all generations.
Awake, awake, put on strength,
  O arm of the Lord!
Awake, as in days of old,
  the generations of long ago!
Was it not you who cut Rahab in pieces,
  who pierced the dragon?
Was it not you who dried up the sea,
  the waters of the great deep;
who made the depths of the sea a way
  for the redeemed to cross over?
So the ransomed of the Lord shall return,
  and come to Zion with singing;
everlasting joy shall be upon their heads;
  they shall obtain joy and gladness,
  and sorrow and sighing shall flee away.

    Isaiah 51:1–11

I consider that the sufferings of this present time are not worth comparing with the glory about to be revealed to us. For the creation waits with eager longing for the revealing of the children of God; for the creation was subjected to futility, not of its own will but by the will of the one who subjected it, in hope that the creation itself will be set free from its bondage to decay and will obtain the freedom of the glory of the children of God. We know that the whole creation has been groaning in labour pains until now; and not only the creation, but we ourselves, who have the first fruits of the Spirit, groan inwardly while we wait for adoption, the redemption of our bodies. For in hope we were saved. Now hope that is seen is not hope. For who hopes for what is seen? But if we hope for what we do not see, we wait for it with patience.

ROMANS 8:18–25

MEDITATION

Ogden Nash once said, "Man is a victim of dope / In the incurable form of hope." Human beings are addicted to hope. When there is a ready supply of hope we remain happy and calm, but the loss of hope is devastating. It is no wonder, then, that so many have thought that hope is a great evil, and that human beings would be better off without it. Robert Ingersoll, for example, quipped that "hope is the only universal liar who never loses his reputation for veracity." And Lord Byron, in savage, sexist imagery, asked, "But what is Hope? Nothing but the paint on the face of Existence; the least touch of truth rubs it off, and then we see what a hollow-cheeked harlot we have got hold of."

The Apostle Paul, by contrast, had a high opinion of hope—not as a virtuous necessity, to mollify the frustrated and restless masses, but as a necessary virtue. In fact, he took hope to be one of the three cardinal virtues—faith, hope, and love—though he thought love was the greatest of the three.

Do disagreements this severe ever bother you? Place Paul's view that hope is a great virtue against, for example, Henry Miller's judgment that "hope is a bad thing. It means that you are not what you want to be. It means that part of you is dead, if not all of you. It means that you entertain illusions. It's a sort of spiritual clap, I should say." Now that's a disagreement of major proportions. Spiritual disease or cardinal virtue? Groundless escapism or powerful motivation for life? Either Miller and his kin have been overcome by cynicism or Paul has succumbed to nonsense. Or maybe both.

In this debate, though not in all debates, I take the side of Paul: hope is a virtue. But ask yourself: what could that mean? How can hope be a virtue? Let us ponder for a moment that greatest of virtues, love. It takes a lifetime of diligent effort for good Methodists and Catholics to cultivate the virtue of love. This process is so difficult that few Presbyterians ever manage it, and Baptists don't even bother with love because for them it is a political liability. The virtue of love doesn't pop out of thin air, but is the result of a serious, patient response to the grace of God in our lives. Well, that is all well and good for love, but how is hope supposed to be cultivated? Don't we either have hope, in which case we have finished before we start, or lose hope, in which case there is nothing left to cultivate? And how are you supposed to cultivate hope if you happen to have some on hand? Hope is easy, when you've got some, isn't it? Our lives are full of hopes, as autumn is full of leaves. Who needs practice?

Actually, love may or may not be virtuous. Floppy-eared, droopy-eyed, puppy love is fun, but not especially virtuous. Overpowering, senses-spinning, erotic love is thrilling, but it is not necessarily virtuous, either. Only love properly understood is virtuous. Thus, we must understand hope properly if we are to understand its possession to be virtuous, if we are to vindicate Paul against the swipes of grim-reaping cultural luminaries.

If our task is to understand hope properly, one step in the right direction might be to ponder a couple of less than perfectly virtuous kinds of hope.

The most obvious sort of virtue-deficient hope is hope-against-hope hope. This is hope without justification; hope with the reason gutted out; empty, desperate, wafting, wistful, wretched wishing. There can be a kind of courage accompanying such groundless hope, and thus it can achieve a kind of nobility, as existentialists affirming the absurdity of the world heroically illustrate. Hope-against-hope hope is hard and heartless, merciless to the ones who hope, leaving them ever longing. It has to be self-consciously generated internally from one's own sense of alienation, and maintained with a kind of detached air that belies the driving nausea beneath the calm surface. This requires a degree of discipline that, frankly, simply cannot be achieved by anyone except the strangest and most brilliant of human beings. The rest of us feel that, as the saying goes, and as our inner cities show, "Take hope from the heart of man and you make him a beast of prey" (the phrase of Ouida, the pseudonym of English novelist Maria Louise Ramé). Most of us would prefer the illusory hope of religious fantasy to the loss of hope if the destruction of civilization were the price. This is the most powerful argument in favor of hope-against-hope hope. It is a genuine sort of hope, and it does have a kind of virtue. It is not, however, the virtuous hope of Christian faith or any other religion.

Another kind of virtue-deficient hope is, to use an Australian idiom, no-worries hope. This is hope without patience, without pain or persistence. It seems more religious than hope-against-hope hope because it makes supernatural, "here comes the divine cavalry" assumptions at its core. But no-worries hope is less virtuous because it short-circuits the struggle to come to terms with ourselves and our possibilities. It is a solution without a problem, triumph without training, resurrection without execution, eternal reward without striving for holiness, Kingdom of God without moral battle. It is, finally, a kind of denial of the difficulty of discerning grounds for hope in the world. Instead of honestly facing the fact that personal transformation, social justice, life after death, and the Kingdom of God are not forgone conclusions, no-worries hope in the face of the storms of life simply lowers the sails, battens down the hatches, drops the anchor, and goes below to drink rum until the agony of life is forgotten in a blissfully unrealistic haze of happy thoughts about calm waters and blue lagoons.

If hope-against-hope hope is reserved for the very few grand-masters of personal discipline, no-worries hope is custom made by and for the multitude of spiritual and moral weaklings. Somewhere between the groundlessness of the one, and the unrealism of the other, if Paul is to be believed, there is a kind of hard-won hope that is rightly called virtuous.

All religious hope begins by noticing what we and our world are like, so as to imagine what we might become. That is partly what revelation is about, for revelation can be understood as the disclosure of what we are not (and so what we can be) through the experience of what we are in the context of the mysterious, divine depth of our being. We need our history and our heritage to do that properly. That's the way the passage from Isaiah develops: "Look to the rock from which you were hewn, and to the quarry from which you were dug. Look to Abraham your father and to Sarah who bore you" (51:1b–2a). This past conditions the self-understanding of the Jews in their years of exile. On that basis, Isaiah imagines a transformed future on their behalf: "So the ransomed of the LORD shall return, and come to Zion with singing; everlasting joy shall be upon their heads; they shall obtain joy and gladness, and sorrow and sighing shall flee away" (51:11). The result is hope. Hope is grounded in the confidence that history can bear the weight of our aspirations for ourselves and our world under God, and this confidence is originally rooted in the revelatory encounter with God in the present. Hope is the effect of revelation projected into the future.

Most religious traditions agree in various ways and words that we are at one level conflicted creatures and bound, and thus they cultivate hope for perfect harmony and freedom. But this experience of disharmony and bondage, once grasped, generates serious religious hope in fundamentally different ways. I am unaware of any arguments that decisively privilege the Christian hope over other ways. But the differences are important.

Some traditional forms of religious hope, having considered our present state, look directly to eternity as perfect harmony or as perfect freedom. After that, history and nature are either secondary but necessary means to attaining that end, or ultimately the delusory product of our conflicted bondage.

Christian religious hope, by contrast, after grasping our situation, next looks ahead into history and nature to understand the possibilities of transformation, and then beyond history and nature to eternity. Thus, Christian hope understands history and nature as alive with transformative possibility. Indeed, hope ultimately subordinates history and nature to the dynamic life of God by projecting the possibility of transformation and fulfillment beyond history and nature. But history and nature preserve their importance in the Christian view of hope because together they constitute the characteristic lens through which eternity presents itself to the imagination informed by Christian symbols. That means that Christians symbolize the object of their hope not in the first instance as the perfectly calm cessation of striving, nor as the attainment of perfect knowledge, but rather as nature perfected, history fulfilled, and humanity reconciled in a new heaven and a new earth in the Kingdom of God.

Of course, there are no decisive arguments for the rational justification of this hope—not in relation to life after death, nor in relation to the overcoming of social strife and injustice, nor in relation to the bleak cosmic future, nor in relation to the intelligibility of the idea of a new heaven and a new earth. The certainty some mature people feel in relation to these matters is relatively rare and usually transitory due to the lack of supportive evidence. These wondrous goals are uncertain, and must remain so. But, then, are they perhaps merely another form of delusory wishing? That can never be ruled out, except by reverting to the no-worries perversion of hope. As Paul says, "hope that is seen is not hope. For who hopes for what is seen? But if we hope for what we do not see, we wait for it with patience" (Rom 8:24–25).

⁂

If *this* is hope, then, why is it *virtuous*? Granted, the virtue of hope does not lie in the certainty of attaining its object. But then what does make this hope virtuous? Surely not merely the avoiding of the extremes of hope-against-hope and no-worries hope. What is the virtuous heart of hope?

This is a genuinely difficult question. Whipping ourselves into a frenzy of enthusiasm about the wonderful objects of the Christian hope—the resurrection of the dead and eternal life, the Kingdom of God and the rule of love and justice—really only evades the difficult question I have raised. We need to plunge into the problematic heart of Christian hope, where inspiration dawns slowly, but lasts all day.

There are only two uses of the words translated "hope" in the gospels. Both are trivial occurrences as part of a parable or a narrative, and do not express anything about the concept of hope. Elsewhere in the New Testament, and in many places in the Old Testament, there is a heavy emphasis on the theme of hope. Is there any significance to this? Perhaps hope doesn't get talked about in the gospels for the same reason that Jesus' disciples didn't fast and pray like John the Baptist's followers did: you don't need to do that kind of thing when Jesus is present. You fast and pray and speak of hope only when Jesus Christ is absent but promised.

The same fundamental point can be seen lurking elsewhere. If hope is grounded in the confidence that history can bear the weight of our aspirations for ourselves and our world under God, and if hope is the effect of revelation projected into the future, then hope depends upon a kind of divinely supported space of possibilities in history and nature, within which it is possible to conceive of personal and social transformation. That is, the premise for speaking of hope in the Christian sense seems to be the reality of God's absence, and the promise of God's presence.

The virtue of hope lies in holding fast to both absence and promise. Divine absence cannot be isolated from divine promise without lapsing into the distortion of hope-against-hope hope. Likewise, promise cannot be spoken of without the implication of absence, which is why its characteristic distortion—no-worries hope—must take the form of a denial of absence. It is far from easy, however, to discern hope in divine absence and promise. It takes discipline and love and longing, initiated by a revelatory disclosure of ourselves in the presence of divine mystery, guided by a worshipping community in which the symbols of eternal hope are treasured, and patiently worked out in practical details that lead to the transformation of lives and social conditions. Thus it is that Christian hope is one of the cardinal virtues.

What do we have when the virtue of hope is practiced in fidelity to the reality of God's absence, and the promise of God's presence?

On the one hand, we have social and political dynamite. Emily Dickinson is famous for the following verse, among other things:

> "Hope" is the thing with feathers—
> That perches in the soul—
> And sings the tunes without the words—
> And never stops—at all—.

There is belligerence in that last line. The supposedly delicate thing with feathers that ought to tire quickly from its frailty, that tiny thing that inspires the soul to a virtuous resolution, that stupid and dull thing that can't even remember the words to the song, that perverse and stubborn thing that can never make good on its own rational basis—that thing, hope, never stops, not ever, not at all.

It's a dangerous, joyous idea. If you are in the business of destroying lives, then watch out, for the dull-edged, unconquerable virtue of hope will finish your reign of terror in the end. If you are in the oppression business, depending on cooperative silence from the weak, then watch out, for the ever-stirring, dynamic virtue of hope will start squawking. If you are committed to accruing wealth for inert shareholders through raping the environment and exploiting low-wage workers, then watch out, for the no-name, no-account virtue of hope has your number and will come calling. Nothing can silence virtuous hope: neither oppression nor poverty, neither disease nor pain, neither terrors of the mind nor ravages of nature, neither violence nor threats of violence, neither disappointment nor desperate longing. Virtuous hope can take the pressure, and keep on singing.

On the other hand, when the virtue of hope is practiced in fidelity to the reality of absence and promise, we have something else along with social and political dynamite. It is delightfully ironic: in and through the dynamic transformation of lives, institutions, nature, and history engendered by hope, we encounter the very thing we most long for—the presence of God. The practice of hope may depend on divine absence and promise, but it discloses divine presence. In this encounter, revelation occurs and the cycle of virtuous hope begins all over again, ever stronger, ever clearer.

This is no word game, for the dynamics of hope are utterly serious. There is only ever divine presence through absence—to affirm otherwise would be tantamount to idolatry. Just as Jesus Christ is, in a famous theologian's wonderful phrase, the divine incognito (Karl Barth), so the virtue of hope is the divine presence *in absentia*. Without promise there can be no hope; without absence there is no need for hope. But as absence and promise join, hope is born, and the divine presence is intimated with almighty power, shading off in all directions into mystery, and absent most obviously precisely at the focus of our attention.

To cultivate the virtue of hope, then, is to practice the presence of God.

God Is ... Monarch

READING

When Samuel became old, he made his sons judges over Israel. The name of his firstborn son was Joel, and the name of his second, Abijah; they were judges in Beer-sheba. Yet his sons did not follow in his ways, but turned aside after gain; they took bribes and perverted justice.

 Then all the elders of Israel gathered together and came to Samuel at Ramah, and said to him, "You are old and your sons do not follow in your ways; appoint for us, then, a king to govern us, like other nations." But the thing displeased Samuel when they said, "Give us a king to govern us." Samuel prayed to the Lord, and the Lord said to Samuel, "Listen to the voice of the people in all that they say to you; for they have not rejected you, but they have rejected me from being king over them. Just as they have done to me, from the day I brought them up out of Egypt to this day, forsaking me and serving other gods, so also they are doing to you. Now then, listen to their voice; only—you shall solemnly warn them, and show them the ways of the king who shall reign over them."

 So Samuel reported all the words of the Lord to the people who were asking him for a king. He said, "These will be the ways of the king who will reign over you: he will take your sons and appoint them to his chariots and to be his horsemen, and to run before his chariots; and he will appoint for himself commanders of thousands and commanders of fifties, and some to plough his ground and to reap his harvest, and to make his implements of war and the equipment of his chariots. He will take your daughters to be perfumers and cooks and bakers. He will take the best of your fields and vineyards and olive orchards and give them to his courtiers. He will take one-tenth of your grain and of your vineyards and give it to his officers and his courtiers. He will take your male and female slaves, and the best of your cattle and donkeys, and put them to his work. He will take one-tenth of your flocks, and you shall be his slaves. And in that day you will cry out because of your king, whom you have chosen for yourselves; but the LORD will not answer you in that day."

But the people refused to listen to the voice of Samuel; they said, "No! but we are determined to have a king over us, so that we also may be like other nations, and that our king may govern us and go out before us and fight our battles." When Samuel had heard all the words of the people, he repeated them in the ears of the LORD. The LORD said to Samuel, "Listen to their voice and set a king over them." Samuel then said to the people of Israel, "Each of you return home."

1 SAMUEL 8:1–22

MEDITATION

The Bible portrays Samuel as a formidable figure, a paragon of virtue, a mine of wisdom, a man with God's ear, no less. He solved one problem after another in the period leading up to the inauguration of monarchy in Israel. The people loved him and trusted his judgment. Under Samuel's judgeship, as the early part of 1 Samuel would have it, Israel had found the ideal political-economic arrangement: a theocracy with a holy man as God's representative—a man faithful to God's wishes who yet somehow managed to hold the goodwill of the people. Now, that's an achievement. The relative peace and quiet between Israel and its neighbors toward the end of Samuel's life was evidence that all was well in the land without a king. The Philistines had been routed and were leaving Israel alone for a while. The dangerous Ark of the Covenant had been returned from Israel's enemies and was being safely handled with appropriate ritual propriety. It was a high point in Israel's history, and it couldn't have happened without God's representative, Samuel.

1 Samuel 8 ushers us into the perspective of this great man. In this story, Samuel is peeved. He is resentful because the people want a king. They still trust him, of course, because they come to him with their complaint. It is Samuel's two sons who are the problem. Samuel had appointed

them judges over Israel, but they proved susceptible to corruption as their power began to attract the ancient equivalent of PAC money and the attention of reasonable people with reasonable arguments seeking reasonable favors. I suppose this must have been one of the few times that Samuel's good judgment had failed. Family succession of judgeship hadn't worked with Eli before Samuel, and it was failing again this time. Holy judges just pop up from God's good earth. Not even Samuel could pass his virtue and wisdom to his children.

Some commentators say that Samuel was righteously indignant because the people were turning their backs on God when they clamored for a king. I don't buy it. Samuel had messed up and his kids had let him down. He's furious. And then the people come to him complaining about his boys as if Samuel, like always, will be patient and wise and solve the problem. Sure enough, Samuel does solve the problem. The Bible even makes a pun out of Samuel's solution: the people asked for it—that's sa-al in Hebrew—and they got sa-ul, King Saul. The story doesn't say what happened to the terrible twosome of Samuel's kids. And it doesn't explain old Samuel's error of judgment either. Maybe he had tried keeping the judgeship within his own family as a hedge against his own death. Who knows? But Samuel was mad at himself as much as he was angry at the people's easy disposal of their precious theocracy.

Let us now take up the perspective of the teller of this story and that of the hypothetical Deuteronomist redactor who got a chance to have some input into the form our text now takes. From the later editorial point of view, the people of Israel, in pleading for a King, were turning their backs on God. The old refrain from Deuteronomy kicks in at verse 8, when Yahweh is made to say, "Just as they have done to me, from the day I brought them up out of Egypt to this day, forsaking me and serving other gods, so also they are doing to you." God is monarch for these people, but in the strict sense that *only* God is monarch. It is not hard to see why a later editor might think that having a second, human monarch is a bad idea. The kingship saga makes for depressing reading. Saul is unstable, David is unfaithful, Solomon breaks the national bank to build the temple, the kingdom splits in the process, and a litany of woe is the result, leading through an almost unbroken series of monarchic failures to the destruction of the northern kingdom by the Assyrians and the eventual overrunning of the southern kingdom by the Babylonians. Israel might have thought it needed a monarchy for military reasons, to dispel the impression of being easy to invade. But the editor wants readers to understand that monarchies in Israel can never work because *only* God is monarch. So when Israel asked for it, they really did get it. At least that's how our hypothetical Deuteronomist redactor saw things.

I think there is something fishy about the Deuteronomistic explanation for the origin of Israelite monarchy. Hindsight is 20/20 for later redactors, but what about the people's point of view in the story for today? They had legitimate gripes. They were being ruled by corrupt judges. They lacked the powerfully unifying symbol of kingship that neighboring nations enjoyed. And Israel's somewhat disorganized form of political life would once again make it seem an easy target to the Philistines, just as soon as the sting of their defeats in Samuel's time had faded. Would you want to live under those conditions? It is easy to imagine the noisy complainers, marching with banners waving, grateful that there was a person like Samuel to turn to in a time of national crisis. The Philistines were an imminent threat. The old system just wasn't working and offered no security in a world that heartlessly runs over people without the means to protect themselves. Samuel was wonderful, but his type was rare. The Israelites weren't rejecting Samuel, no matter what he felt about the situation. Nor were they rejecting God as their king when they asked for a human king of their own. They were merely begging God to act like a king, to take care of his own.

What should *we* think about this story? We have ventured to see it from Samuel's and from the people's points of view, and we have tried to figure out what was important to its writers and redactors. But the truth is, the origin of kingship in Israel is an extraordinarily complicated historical matter. At some point we have to look beyond the intricate historical foliage and take in a larger view. This passage from 1 Samuel helps us do that by offering potent insights into the nature of human political and social life, and by helping us construct a profound conception of divine monarchy.

Let us reflect for a moment on the final verse of this chapter: "The Lord said to Samuel, 'Listen to their voice and set a king over them.' Samuel then said to the people of Israel, 'Each of you return home.'" Now, why would Samuel say that? He might as well have said, "OK, OK, you can have your king. And don't forget the Women's Fellowship bingo night next Tuesday." It seems to me to be a giant non-sequitur. Why say "Go home"? Scholars have lots of interpretations of Samuel's outburst, and their diversity invites us to speculate. So let's speculate. In fact, let's do more than speculate; let's project the deepest possible meaning on the text.

Telling the people to go home is telling them to calm down; it is reassuring them that everything will be all right; it is admonishing them not to cause trouble. It recognizes their anxiety about the future and lets them know that God will take care of them. It is a grand literary symbol for an epochal shift in a nation's consciousness: the leaving behind of political innocence and the necessary embrace of the complexities of all manner of social and political institutions. In my projected version of that verse, Samuel is sighing. He is unable to protect his beloved people from harsh social realities any longer, and he silently allows his people to slip into the twilight zone of the unending complexities and the intriguing possibilities of national political institutions.

Now, Israel was never innocent of institutional realities. Nevertheless, there is a kind of fall story being told here: a fall from the impossible innocence of theocracy mediated by a trusted, holy judge to the reality of messy societies and half-effective institutions, the very same reality that we know to be ours, the world of power and compromise that has been the lot of our species ever since we started trying to live together in big groups.

We humans share deep instincts to protect ourselves from the vagaries of life, to band together to hold off the night, to pool resources to get things done. For our prehistoric ancestors this was a primal yearning to belong to a group in which they could be relatively safe, to mate and to eat. We have that same yearning, but for us it also involves a never-ending quest for institutional forms that can extend our ability to control our environment, that can carry wisdom and knowledge into the future, that can create light switches, pipe organs, computers, and choral music.

We need our institutions—both the social, political, and economic patterns of organization that help us to survive, and the educational and cultural structures that help us to thrive. We have to invest ourselves in them, take responsibility for them, improve and transform them. Institutions are

God Is . . . Monarch

God's gift to social creatures. They represent our chance to realize our most adventurous dreams of stable life conditions, safe communities, healthy bodies, just societies, wise and happy children, powerful ideas, glorious sculptures, and the simple pleasures of clean water and nutritious food. Institutions are a great blessing.

At the same time, however, institutions are a great curse. It is institutions that allow individual corruption to congeal into the crud of poisonous political depravity. It is institutions that permit charismatic charlatans to achieve power equal to their wildest dreams, often with devastating consequences. It is institutions that lock us into patterns of economic exploitation that force us to make despicable, no-win choices between economic well-being and caring for widows and orphans. It is institutions that magnify the paranoia of weak individuals to the point that torture and mass killings become—God help us all—the *rational* way to preserve political stability. It is institutions that carelessly trample individuals underfoot on the way to accomplishing more important goals. Institutions—you can't live with 'em, you can't live without 'em.

The fact is that institutions are an inevitable part of our lives, every bit as much a part of creation as flowers and people, viruses and sports. If we read this passage from 1 Samuel carelessly, we may be driven to deny this. Or we might be tempted to conclude that there is a perfect institutional form, realizable with appropriate work and wisdom. Heaven help us all if we fall for those traps. There is nothing worse than anti-institutional separatists and political zealots when the rest of us are trying to take care of business. On the contrary, we need to be political realists and, as Reinhold Niebuhr put it, Christian realists. We need to remember that God is monarch. And we must never forget the double-edged character of that idea.

On the one hand, to say that God is monarch means that God is our monarch. God is the one to whom we defer as the ruler and protector of each one of us, our families, our communities, our societies, our nations, our species, and our biosphere, and every wider sphere of reality beyond that. And God is the one to whom we rightly complain when things go wrong. We speak of divine monarchy as a way of reminding ourselves that our institutions can be the means of God's loving provision for us and for others, that all of the institutions of which we are a part can trace the lineage of their mandate back to heaven.

On the other hand, to say that God is monarch is, as it was for the ancient Israelites, a potent reminder that all of our institutions are relativized in the presence of God, that every institution born in our history will need to be renewed. How easy it is to utter those words. But consider how difficult and costly it is to embrace the task they define! To take a prophetic stance against institutional corruption is like punching a billion pillows, and if you ever hit something hard you are likely to become the victim of character assassination or worse. Institutionally sanctioned evils from racism to plain old greed have caused the death of prophets over and over again. The Christian martyrs went to their deaths singing the praises of the One who gives the very institutions that torment and kill, and those martyrs died for the sake of the right to realize in those institutions the freedom each individual bears within his or her soul to worship God. The martyrs of all times and places have died at the hands of heartless, blood-thirsty, or ignorant representatives of institutions, and yet their deaths were often the very seeds that flourished into the eventual transformation of those same institutions.

The Christian understanding of divine monarchy achieves its most profound and perplexing expression in the person of Jesus the Christ. With incredible boldness, the Christian tradition centralized this figure as a symbol of both divine power and divine love: Christ the king is Christ crucified. The casual execution of this man at the hands of a massive, bureaucratized political institution gave birth in turn to a renegade institution that celebrates him as its paradoxical king—and this infant institution eventually became the skeletal framework into which the great Roman structure collapsed. In this way the Graeco-Roman cultural heritage was preserved even after the empire's political identity had disintegrated.

What a strange form of divine monarchy we celebrate, one that creates and destroys our institutions in the tides of history, one that renders them unavoidable and yet demands our commitment on their behalf, one that calls us both to their cultivation and their critique, one that takes for its hero an abandoned prophet whose message is institutional dynamite and whose death gave way to renewed life for us all.

God Is … Wisdom

READINGS

The heavens are telling the glory of God;
    and the firmament proclaims his handiwork.
Day to day pours forth speech,
    and night to night declares knowledge.
There is no speech, nor are there words;
    their voice is not heard;
yet their voice goes out through all the earth,
    and their words to the end of the world.
In the heavens he has set a tent for the sun,
which comes out like a bridegroom from his wedding canopy,
    and like a strong man runs its course with joy.
Its rising is from the end of the heavens,
    and its circuit to the end of them;
    and nothing is hidden from its heat.
The law of the Lord is perfect,
    reviving the soul;
the decrees of the Lord are sure,
    making wise the simple;
the precepts of the Lord are right,
    rejoicing the heart;
the commandment of the Lord is clear,
    enlightening the eyes;
the fear of the Lord is pure,

God Is . . .

enduring for ever;
the ordinances of the Lord are true
   and righteous altogether.
More to be desired are they than gold,
   even much fine gold;
sweeter also than honey,
   and drippings of the honeycomb.
Moreover by them is your servant warned;
   in keeping them there is great reward.
But who can detect their errors?
   Clear me from hidden faults.
Keep back your servant also from the insolent;
   do not let them have dominion over me.
Then I shall be blameless,
   and innocent of great transgression.
Let the words of my mouth and the meditation of my heart
   be acceptable to you,
     O Lord, my rock and my redeemer.
        Psalm 19

Wisdom cries out in the street;
   in the squares she raises her voice.
At the busiest corner she cries out;
   at the entrance of the city gates she speaks:
"How long, O simple ones, will you love being simple?
How long will scoffers delight in their scoffing
   and fools hate knowledge?
Give heed to my reproof;
I will pour out my thoughts to you;
   I will make my words known to you.
Because I have called and you refused,
   have stretched out my hand and no one heeded,
and because you have ignored all my counsel
   and would have none of my reproof,
I also will laugh at your calamity;
   I will mock when panic strikes you,

when panic strikes you like a storm,
  and your calamity comes like a whirlwind,
  when distress and anguish come upon you.
Then they will call upon me, but I will not answer;
  they will seek me diligently, but will not find me.
Because they hated knowledge
  and did not choose the fear of the Lord,
would have none of my counsel,
  and despised all my reproof,
therefore they shall eat the fruit of their way
  and be sated with their own devices.
For waywardness kills the simple,
  and the complacency of fools destroys them;
but those who listen to me will be secure
  and will live at ease, without dread of disaster."

PROVERBS 1:20–33

Not many of you should become teachers, my brothers and sisters, for you know that we who teach will be judged with greater strictness.

JAMES 3:1

Then he began to teach them that the Son of Man must undergo great suffering, and be rejected by the elders, the chief priests, and the scribes, and be killed, and after three days rise again. He said all this quite openly. And Peter took him aside and began to rebuke him. But turning and looking at his disciples, he rebuked Peter and said, "Get behind me, Satan! For you are setting your mind not on divine things but on human things."

He called the crowd with his disciples, and said to them, "If any want to become my followers, let them deny themselves and take up their cross and follow me. For those who want to save their life will lose it, and those who lose their life for my sake, and for the sake of the gospel, will save it. For what will it profit them to gain the whole world and forfeit their life?"

MARK 8:31–36

God Is . . .

MEDITATION

Every language has areas of semantic intensity, places where an enormous richness of vocabulary allows us, in the right context, to express virtually every nuance of meaning we can imagine. These areas of language are much used and greatly needed in our day-to-day life, for life's complexities demand subtle tailoring of meanings.

Consider, for example, and quite hypothetically, the task of venting our fury at incompetent drivers. We could shout "fool", of course, but that lacks color and thus inhibits the venting. In English, however, as well as in most European languages, there are oodles of alternatives: chump, imbecile, jackass, clod, moron, booby, loser, jerk, and dope, to name but a few. We can also team words up together with amazing variety to vent our spleen, as in featherhead, emptyhead, blockhead, dunderhead, wisehead, saphead, softhead, pinhead, birdbrain, featherbrain, lamebrain, scatterbrain, rattlebrain, dumbbell, lightweight, and ninnyhammer.

Recalling that all this is utterly hypothetical, because none of us would abuse our fellow drivers, we may note still more alternatives from ways of impugning intelligence—cretin, dimwit, dolt, dullard, halfwit, and idiot—to creative application of animal names—donkey, flounder, goose, monkey, rabbit, pigeon, and ape. There is a vast class of relatively offensive equivalents for our bland "fool" that cannot be repeated here, as well as national preferences, as in Australia's favorites: gallah, ninny, nitwit, twerp, twit, and dope. And then there are still other ways of saying "fool" without actually using the word, ways for every occasion and every taste: bungler, buffoon, cull, doodle, dummy, dunce, dupe, easymark, fallguy, feeb, flake, gudgeon, gull, idler, ignoramus, jester, laughingstock, madman, mark, motley, mug, nincompoop, numskull, patsy, poop, pushover, sap, schmo, schmuck, simpleton, sucker, tomfool, trifle, windbag, wiseacre, wisecrack, and wiseguy.

Evidently, we are well equipped in English to handle fools, and I'll wager that almost every living language is similar. And now, lest you think me absurd, asinine, balmy, cracked, demented, crazy, deranged, doddering, daffy, dilly, dippey, or dotty, let me hasten to make my point. After all, to spend so much time on an introduction in a brief meditation would be foolish—or should I say halfcocked, halfwitted, frivolous, fatuous, imbecilic, imprudent, inane, insane, jerky, kooky, loopy, loony, nutty, potty, stupid, silly, wacky, wild, sappy, zany, and daft.

God Is . . . Wisdom

The point is this: we seem fascinated by wisdom and especially the lack of it. The verbal blizzard you have just heard discloses our interest in wisdom, our need to accuse people who lack it, and the myriad ways we do, in fact, prove to be unwise, or foolish, each day.

Hebrew wisdom literature, of which the book of Proverbs is an instance, is likewise fascinated by wisdom. In fact, the great sages whose aphoristic teachings are recorded in Proverbs were intrigued by wisdom and personified it as a woman—and this metaphor became a hard-working literary device at the hands of the post-exilic editors who gave the book its final form. Most of us are fascinated by wisdom, by the traces it leaves in our languages, by its importance in each one of our lives. I feel the same urge to personalize wisdom that the Hebrew sages knew, because nothing but personal imagery seems able to capture the vividness, fluid grace, and practicality of wisdom. So woman wisdom it shall be for me, also.

The Proverbs reading introduces the figure of woman wisdom. The central point of the passage is a simple one: having wisdom, paying attention to her, matters. "The complacency of fools destroys them; but those who listen to me will be secure and will live at ease, without dread of disaster" (32b–33). Notice in passing a subtle theological point here: rather than settling for saying that those who listen to wisdom "will be secure and will live at ease," the verse carefully glosses being at ease as being "without dread of disaster." That implicitly acknowledges that disasters can befall everyone, even the wise. The advantage possessed by the wise involves dignity and freedom from dread. Of course, the wise avoid doing the stupid things that get them killed, too; "for waywardness kills the simple" (32a).

Most people understand that wisdom matters. We may even agree with the sages that we have to work hard to become wise, and that wisdom cannot be produced from out of thin air when disaster strikes and causes universal panic. All of this is obvious, after all, isn't it? So we are all very wise.

There is great danger here. We must face down an awkward question to avoid a bland and boring escape from the challenge of this reading from Proverbs: Who are the fools to which the passage refers—the scoffers, the simple ones, the refusers, the ignorers, the haters of knowledge, the ones who choose not the fear of the Lord, the ones who panic when disaster strikes? Who are they whose dreadful punishment is to be abandoned to what they want, to what they stupidly, dully seek for themselves? Who are they that are damned to be "sated by their own devices" (31b), their cars and jobs, their families and leisure, their social work and prayers? Well, to cut to the chase, you know I must mean that the fools are us. But that's OK, because you think I am just speaking rhetorically; it doesn't cost us anything to admit politely that we are fools, in a certain sense, relative to woman wisdom in the great gray ocean of ambiguity that washes away all our iniquities.

We are such sneaky readers of the Bible. Nothing sticks when we have enough church experience to slide teflon-clean through biblical challenges. C'mon Bible, bring on the worst you've got. Call me a sinner, a fool, a refuser of wisdom. I can take it. I can take it because I just turn off my brain and let my emotions sweep me into mindless agreement. I can take it because I know it's all just a way of speaking and it doesn't really mean what it says. I can take it because secretly I disagree with it. Well, to heck with slippery evasions. To heck with slick rationalizations and emotional indulgences. The Bible says we are in desperate danger because we have an ingrained tendency to be fools. It says we don't realize this danger because we don't notice it until disaster strikes, and then it is too late. Each of us can decree ourselves the exception that makes the rule if we like, but I tell you, I will not. I have this damnable tendency, this disease of foolishness whose penalty is to be left alone with all we averagely wanted. The Bible is right about me and I bet it is right about you too.

So far, I hope you realize, I haven't given you any reasons to believe me. All I have tried to do is to unmask our carefully cultivated habits of listening with teflon ears. But I want you to believe me, so let me give some examples.

Many of you may not have thought much about what it is like to be a professor in a college or university. Teachers, of course, are experts in their areas of specialty and some are world leaders at the precise thing they do best. But most teachers are fairly practical people, even if you can't always tell that from their classes. Most have hidden talents. And most care about their students and feel privileged to teach them. But teachers also have their own characteristic form of foolishness. They tend to forget. They forget James' dictum that "we who teach will be judged with greater strictness" (3:1). They see generations of students come and go and forget what coming to college must feel like. They give classes year after year and forget that student learning matters more than their teaching. They forget to treasure every ounce of their students' enthusiasm because as experienced teachers they have seen it all before and they have seen time change everything. They forget their own first love of their chosen field of expertise because they can't afford to remember the kind of blazing fire that upsets impeccable academic judgment. They forget that woman wisdom slips through the fingers of the half-hearted grasp because their hands always seem to come back from their reaching full of something worthwhile. They forget for the same reason that everyone forgets as they get older: it is exhausting to stay fresh, and it is arduous to look at similar things year after year with the attention required to sense the glory of each individual. They are in danger of getting what they want, of being "sated on their own devices," of being judged strictly because they foolishly forgot too long and too often.

The reading from Mark is a particularly colorful and punchy story in that most colorful and punchy of gospels. Peter has just finished declaring that Jesus is the Messiah. Mark presents Peter's declaration as a stroke of theological genius. But next thing you know, Jesus calls him Satan and accuses Peter of worrying about human rather than divine things. Maybe Peter just got lucky with his Messiah answer. But he sure was confident. I used to have a mathematics professor who would force our tiny class to vote on alternative answers to a conceptually tricky question. Sometimes I was the only one right and sometimes I was the only one wrong, but often I was voting alone. I wonder how Peter felt about voting alone so often. What must it have been like to be the insightful one who figures out that Jesus is the Messiah? Or the Satan who tries to talk Jesus out of a crazy plan? Peter trusted in his judgment so much, but he was more foolish than he knew.

We are all in danger of making Peter's mistake, of trusting in what we know, in what we think is wise, and hastily criticizing what might seem shocking. What we encounter in daily life may well seem shocking sometimes, even when nobody is actually trying to shock us. We quickly reach for a confident proclamation and, before we know it, we are unmasked as fools. When we have the urge to critique something surprising, or praise something unexpected, we should remember Peter's rash overconfidence and try not to make the same mistake. We should critique from curiosity and passion, but not from desperation or fear, nor from a false sense of our own religious wisdom.

To follow Jesus on the path of wisdom, in Mark's words, requires us to deny ourselves, to take up our crosses, and to follow. The path of wisdom for all of us involves those three steps. But becoming wise can't be broken into a three-step recipe. We seek wisdom because we love her, and we fell in love with her for the same intangible reasons that we always fall in love. We don't know where the path will lead us, but the fierce purity of our yearning for woman wisdom lights the way. On that path we discover the grace to admit our foolishness, to surrender our confidence that we must be as right as Peter thought he was. As we walk we allow ourselves to see all around us in new ways, fresh and detailed even in their familiarity. In this way we shoulder the heavy burden of striving after fidelity to wisdom, never settling for today's confidence, forever accepting the risk of being vessels of constant change, learning to be energized by the dynamic life of wisdom herself. Then, placing one foot in front of another, we devote ourselves to the path, in the name of Jesus who walks before and behind us, Jesus the wisdom of God, woman wisdom's own offspring.

God Is . . . Coming

READINGS

O that you would tear open the heavens and come down,
  so that the mountains would quake at your presence—
as when fire kindles brushwood
  and the fire causes water to boil—
to make your name known to your adversaries,
  so that the nations might tremble at your presence!
When you did awesome deeds that we did not expect,
  you came down, the mountains quaked at your presence.
From ages past no one has heard,
  no ear has perceived,
no eye has seen any God besides you,
  who works for those who wait for him.
You meet those who gladly do right,
  those who remember you in your ways.
But you were angry, and we sinned;
  because you hid yourself we transgressed.
We have all become like one who is unclean,
  and all our righteous deeds are like a filthy cloth.
We all fade like a leaf,
  and our iniquities, like the wind, take us away.
There is no one who calls on your name,
  or attempts to take hold of you;

for you have hidden your face from us,
   and have delivered us into the hand of our iniquity.
Yet, O Lord, you are our Father;
   we are the clay, and you are our potter;
   we are all the work of your hand.
Do not be exceedingly angry, O Lord,
   and do not remember iniquity for ever.
   Now consider, we are all your people.

      Isaiah 64:1–9

But in those days, after that suffering,
the sun will be darkened,
and the moon will not give its light,
and the stars will be falling from heaven,
and the powers in the heavens will be shaken.

Then they will see "the Son of Man coming in clouds" with great power and glory. Then he will send out the angels, and gather his elect from the four winds, from the ends of the earth to the ends of heaven.

"From the fig tree learn its lesson: as soon as its branch becomes tender and puts forth its leaves, you know that summer is near. So also, when you see these things taking place, you know that he is near, at the very gates. Truly I tell you, this generation will not pass away until all these things have taken place. Heaven and earth will pass away, but my words will not pass away.

"But about that day or hour no one knows, neither the angels in heaven, nor the Son, but only the Father. Beware, keep alert; for you do not know when the time will come. It is like a man going on a journey, when he leaves home and puts his slaves in charge, each with his work, and commands the doorkeeper to be on the watch. Therefore, keep awake—for you do not know when the master of the house will come, in the evening, or at midnight, or at cockcrow, or at dawn, or else he may find you asleep when he comes suddenly. And what I say to you I say to all: Keep awake."

      Mark 13:24–37

MEDITATION

Advent is the season when the church prepares for Christmas, which is the celebration of God coming in Christ. Of course, Advent is dominated by other kinds of activities, especially shopping for gifts, cooking fine meals, eating more than we should, and schedules jammed with parties. With most people running up steep credit card bills they can't pay, and extra poundage they can't afford, it is a sign of divine providence that Lent, the season of repentance and discipline, arrives each year fairly soon after Christmas.

I was in China last Christmas season and saw a surprising expression of the meaning of Advent. It is slightly mind-bending so I have to explain. The Chinese are an independent people with the kind of confidence that allows them to adapt good ideas from other cultures. Their favorite western cultural creation is Christmas and they have adopted it with a passion. The Chinese version of Advent and Christmas has nothing to do with Christ or the baby Jesus or religion. For kids it is about beautifully wrapped presents. For adults it means several weeks of fun and parties. Everywhere you go you see statues of a western-looking Santa Claus. Most shops show his bearded, smiling face on cardboard cutouts taped to the window. Public places play Christmas music—I heard the Smurfs, as well as Alvin and the Chipmunks—but all secular music, no Christmas carols.

Ask yourself this. If you were a church leader trying to educate your people about Advent in a context like this, how might you do it? In cold, cold Harbin, home of the spectacular International Snow and Ice Festival, I saw how one church did it. The sanctuary of this church was adorned with a large mural of Santa Claus arriving on a sleigh, complete with red-nosed reindeer and a bulging bag of gorgeous gifts. The message was simple: God's coming to us in Christ is just like Santa Claus coming to us at Christmas. In our context, Santa Claus is often a distraction from the spiritual point of Advent. In this Chinese church, Santa Claus was the key to understanding the meaning of God's coming.

We can think of God coming to us in Christ as a beautiful gift. We all need to rehear that message loud and clear at some point in each Advent season. But the Bible also confronts us with a very different message. In this strand of the advent story, God comes in difficult, disturbing ways, unexpected and perhaps even unwelcome. The colors of this coming are not the bright reds and celebratory greens of Santa Claus and laughing children but the dark hues of dawning disaster, of danger and devastation.

God Is . . .

The Isaiah reading has God punishing God's own chosen people for their betrayal. The punishment takes the form of destruction at the hands of foreign nations. According to the prophet, God's people got what they deserved: "You have hidden your face from us, and have delivered us into the hand of our iniquity." God's punishment is not divine absence; far from it. It is the fierce visage of divine wrath, directed at God's own servants. Nothing could be more dismaying, more terrifying. Isaiah is begging God to pick on someone else, to turn the divine wrath toward Isaiah's enemies and to claim the prophet's people once again as God's own. Isaiah's prayer is essentially this: "Please come, O God, but please come to our enemies, and stop punishing us!"

The reading from Mark's gospel is even less cheery. God's coming will be very soon, it says, but you don't know precisely when, so you have to be prepared for anything. There will be signs that God's coming is imminent, and they are all grim omens of cosmic disaster: a blackened sun, a darkened moon, and stars falling from the sky. All this made sense in the cosmology of Mark's day. The heavens were a multi-layered arching shell hosting an epic cosmic drama, often keyed into earthly events. On this view, it is the underworld that is at the center of the universe, not human life, and there is no way to repair and consummate the creation without the dark powers of the underworld showing their faces in calculated resistance. God's righteous armies can and will defeat the power of evil but it is very important that we are on God's side when the chaos goes down. So be ready!

In both of these passages, God is portrayed as powerful and just and deadly, capable of vast anger and great revenge and terrible violence. This God would not hesitate to destroy with vast waves and wild winds and fierce fire, and the cause would always be just because God declares it is just! Nobody is in a position to question God's sense of justice. Trifle with this God at your peril!

It is no wonder that Pat Robertson and other firebrand clerics of the Christian right claim biblical warrant for saying that God sends disasters to punish wickedness. Various among them have said that 9/11 was divine punishment for a wicked nation gone astray, that the 2004 Indian Ocean tsunami was divine punishment for wicked Muslims in Southeast Asia, that the 2005 hurricane Katrina was divine punishment for wicked gays and gamblers in New Orleans, and that the Dover, Pennsylvania, school district can expect God's wrath for wickedly voting in the recent election to throw out the school board members who tried to pass Intelligent Design off as science in order to give it a hearing in science classrooms. Everything means something in a world under God's providential control. The purveyors of this view insist that, if you look at things the way they do, you will see that even the most horrible events make sense. And they promise divine favor and protection for the righteous, so nothing bad will happen to you so long as you remain faithful.

The readings from Isaiah and Mark suggest that this view has at least some biblical support. The biblical God is heavily involved in the punishment and reward business, and nothing happens without this God's permission. God's advent in this scheme of things is often terrifying and reminds us that we need to repent or else suffer and die some more until we change our minds.

Jumping to the other end of the theological spectrum for a moment, it is when we recognize that the biblical God is not necessarily our good buddy that religious liberals can go bananas. They begin by ignoring these difficult biblical passages because they prefer God as a loving, gentle person who wouldn't hurt a flea. They continue by rejecting the idea that God's providence embraces all events, because they don't want God involved in earthquakes and hurricanes. Unfortunately, they end up with a loving God who seems to do nothing of any consequence.

On this issue, many moderate Christians feel caught in the middle with friends and enemies on both sides. We are nauseated by the picture of a friendly, impotent God. Upon reflection, it is a suspiciously WASPy, suburban sort of divine reality. But we are also horrified by the picture of a God who personally and deliberately inflicts unimaginable suffering on the guilty and innocent alike, allegedly to educate wayward human beings. The first God is a useless effigy, a semi-biblical fiction, and a modern creation whose main function is to increase the comfort of comfortable middle-class Christians who already have good healthcare, good nutrition, and good jobs. The second God is a semi-biblical distortion, a cruel master who is too stupid to realize that people never learn how to be truly good from disasters and disease. They only learn how to suffer and die.

We wind up with these disastrous images because we habitually break the very first of the Ten Commandments: we get deeply attached to images of God instead of to the real thing.

Theistic religion routinely presses the limits of the first commandment by making God much like a human being. Of course, the personalities of this divine personal being are wildly divergent—one comes to us as a loving and gentle and patient presence, while the other is ruthless and just and easily upset. But we understand both personalities because they are a lot like us.

The Bible encourages personal imagery for God by using it a lot. Such imagery is anthropomorphic, which literally means "humanly shaped," so we need to be wary of it, just as the first commandment says. But there is an art to using these sorts of images. We can deepen our connection with God using all kinds of images and at the same time remember not to get overly attached to any one of them.

Most theists intuitively practice this art. They make subtle moves with their God images, shifting among them as the situation dictates. They pray to God as a loving parent but don't rush in with that image when it comes time to explain why a child was stricken with cancer. Rather, they speak of the mysterious ways of God in the chances of nature. They accept that God is judge of their souls but don't wave judgment in the faces of people whose homes have been destroyed by a hurricane. They instinctively grasp that God comes in many ways and forms, sometimes like a loving person, sometimes like a severe judge, sometimes like a principle of rational order, sometimes like a mysterious healing force, sometimes like a fickle wind—all biblical images. The unimaginative skeptic may woodenly insist that these adjustments merely save face and mask a lack of conviction. But the whole sweep of the Bible insists that God's coming, God's advent, is multifaceted and hard to pin down. And that's because God's nature is beyond neat description.

Many atheists reject God because, at root, they are appalled by anthropomorphic ideas of God and know of no convincing alternatives. Atheism lies just beneath the polished surface of anthropomorphism. If disaster or disease scratch that surface, human-shaped pictures of God can become suddenly unbelievable. More people go to church in times of disaster but they don't stay—probably because some really don't like what they hear. A

God who personally and deliberately inflicts apparently senseless suffering should be resisted, surely, rather than worshipped. And a God who just smiles and hugs and never does anything useful should be ignored as irrelevant, not adored and served. For the atheist, it makes more sense to say that God just does not exist and then set about making the world a better place. I admire this kind of atheism for its moral clarity and courage of conviction. Yet it is in thrall to the human images of God it rejects every bit as much as the views it dismisses as religious fantasies.

There is a more profound way to think about God's coming, God's advent. With the Bible's prohibitions on idolatry in mind, we can graciously accept the atheist's critique when we make God in our own image. We can refuse the idea of a God who comes to us by intentionally inflicting injury and death. We can repudiate the image of a God who comes to us always and only to make us feel good. We can reject the picture of God as a time-bound being who exists like we exist and thinks sequentially and intentionally like we think.

We can also courteously insist that our atheist friends should look deeper with us. We can follow the trail of bread crumbs in the Bible and other sacred religious texts toward an idea of God as totally other, beyond the comprehension of finite beings, beyond even the categories of existence and non-existence. This God comes to us in the surging creativity of nature and culture, and in the moral steel of the prophet's spine. This God comes in the storm and the rainbow, in the fury of nature's destruction and in the compassionate hands that reach out to help.

God seems untamed when the divine coming harms us. God seems rational when science opens up for us the beautiful patterns of nature. God seems loving when we have cause to be thankful for the breath of life. In all things, however, God is. "I AM" was the way God answered Moses' request for a divine name. In a religious landscape dominated by inane Gods of love and biased Gods of violence, we badly need this robust theism. We need to be confronted by the God beyond Gods, the God who grounds all beings, the God who flows through all creativity. This God comes not as slave to our special interests but as nature's sharp chances and the stunning statements of civilizations.

At advent we recall that this God also came in Christ. Christ is the property of no religion and the possession of no person, but rather friend of all who seek God's Kingdom. To follow Christ is to commit to making God's Kingdom come, on earth as it is in heaven. Just as God comes to us in Christ, so God comes to us when we devote ourselves to Christ-like service in the Kingdom of God. This is a hard and high calling. God's coming confronts us with the challenge to serve where the need is overwhelming, to love where kindness seems lost. God's advent is a true adventure for the one who follows Christ.

But why bother working to realize the Kingdom of God when, to believe Mark's gospel, the world will only get worse and then collapse in flaming cosmic chaos as God's coming destroys everything? Is not God's advent more about our escape from the coming terror than about creating heaven on earth? Why should we care about the environment or nuclear weapons or even world peace? I confess that I do not take literally the Bible's end-of-the-world talk, even though I know that our living planetary home will eventually die, hopefully a long time from now. But even those who do think that God will burst into the world to set things right are obliged to work hard toward the realization the Kingdom of God on earth. That's because the apocalypse might not be all sweetness and light for us. Let me explain.

Surveys show that the large majority of people believe they are more intelligent, more beautiful, and more moral than average. The religious version of this phenomenon of rosy self-perception is that most of us believe we have nothing to fear from God's advent. That's because most of us think God is on our side. Yet surely it is dangerous to be certain that God is on our side. We forget all too easily that Isaiah presents God as coming in judgment to Isaiah's people, to God's own chosen people, to God's favorites. The Bible is full of stories that drive home the point: being on God's side does not mean that God is on our side.

True believers who are absolutely certain that God is on their side and against their enemies are the most dangerous of our brothers and sisters. Extremist Christian clerics can say that the devastating 2008 Pakistan earthquake is God's judgment upon Muslims who shield Osama bin Laden from justice. Extremist Islamic clerics can praise Hurricane Katrina for its role in furthering God's plan to bring the United States to its knees. Both sides are calling God down upon their enemies, just as the Isaiah passage does. This is the grown-up version of the paradox of school football: we pray for our side, they pray for their side, and together we put God in a difficult position. In the grown-up version, God is faced with short-sighted, narrow-minded ideologues who would rather destroy one another out of pride and anger than see their enemies the way God does. Therefore, divine intervention, God's coming, may not go the way we expect.

Despite all the biblical warnings, there is no shortage of people looking forward to the end of the world, just as the church community of Mark's gospel did at one point. The juggernaut "Left Behind" series of novels has created an industry of spin-offs, from movies to comics to T-shirts, all hinging on the unstated premise that we should welcome the final apocalypse because we can know in advance for certain that we'll be just fine when God finally comes to destroy the devil, save the good, and punish the wicked. I am not an enraptured end-of-the-world enthusiast. But I do have a question for those who are: Are they really sure they want God to come? If the Bible is any indication, it will probably turn out that they are at least partly on the wrong side of the divine wrath. If the chosen people of God can wind up out of God's favor, then surely we can.

We are not ready for God's coming! We should beg God not to come, to take a holiday, to give us an extension on our assignment. And in the time that we have, we should prepare. Things are in bad shape down here, and truly horrible for many people on this shrinking planet of ours.

That's why we must remember at advent that God comes not only in cosmic consummation and in the Christ child but also in the challenge to serve. To be part of the Christian movement is to follow Christ's example, to show that the Kingdom of God is at hand by realizing it with our very own hands. God's coming, you see, is our calling. The divine advent is our adventure. We do not know how much time we have. And we can never be sure that God is completely on our side. But we can humbly venture to serve God with all our heart and mind and strength.

We can learn to give God's coming a concrete translation in our own lives. We can love more truly, live more simply, care more deeply, fight more fairly. We can avoid self-righteousness. We can assume that God may be partly on our enemy's side as well as on ours. We can resist the temptation to make God into an image of our own values and character. We can work for the Kingdom of God while we wait for the Kingdom to come.

God Is... Death

READING

For everything there is a season, and a time for every matter under heaven:
 a time to be born, and a time to die;
 a time to plant, and a time to pluck up what is planted;
 a time to kill, and a time to heal;
 a time to break down, and a time to build up;
 a time to weep, and a time to laugh;
 a time to mourn, and a time to dance;
 a time to throw away stones, and a time to gather stones together;
 a time to embrace, and a time to refrain from embracing;
 a time to seek, and a time to lose;
 a time to keep, and a time to throw away;
 a time to tear, and a time to sew;
 a time to keep silence, and a time to speak;
 a time to love, and a time to hate;
 a time for war, and a time for peace.

What gain have the workers from their toil? I have seen the business that God has given to everyone to be busy with. He has made everything suitable for its time; moreover, he has put a sense of past and future into their minds, yet they cannot find out what God has done from the beginning to the end. I know that there is nothing better for them than to be happy and enjoy themselves as long as they live; moreover, it is God's gift that all should eat and drink and take pleasure in all their toil. I know that whatever God does endures for ever; nothing can be added to it, nor anything taken from it; God has done this, so that all should stand in awe before him. That which is, already has been; that which is to be, already is; and God seeks out what has gone by.

Moreover, I saw under the sun that in the place of justice, wickedness was there, and in the place of righteousness, wickedness was there as well. I said in my heart, God will judge the righteous and the wicked, for he has appointed a time for every matter, and for every work. I said in my heart with regard to human beings that God is testing them to show that they are but animals. For the fate of humans and the fate of animals is the same; as one dies, so dies the other. They all have the same breath, and humans have no advantage over the animals; for all is vanity. All go to one place; all are from the dust, and all turn to dust again. Who knows whether the human spirit goes upwards and the spirit of animals goes downwards to the earth? So I saw that there is nothing better than that all should enjoy their work, for that is their lot; who can bring them to see what will be after them?

ECCLESIASTES 3

MEDITATION

[This was a sermon delivered on April 25, 2007, immediately after the Virginia Tech shootings on April 16, 2007, within a Boston University School of Theology worship service devoted to the memory of former colleague Simon Parker who died in tragic circumstances on April 29, 2006, one of a series of faculty deaths; it was also ANZAC Day, which is important to any Australian or New Zealander. This context is important for understanding the sermon.]

Shortly after I arrived at Boston University, I attended a philosophy of science colloquium. I cannot remember what the topic was—probably something obscure like the concept of statistical laws in quantum physics—but I do remember feeling sure that it would be of no interest to my colleagues in the School of Theology or the Religion Department. Imagine my surprise when Simon Parker, Professor of Hebrew Bible and Ancient Near Eastern Languages and Cultures, walked into the room and sat down beside me. I asked him afterwards why he was there and he replied simply that he was curious. As I came to know him better, I realized how very curious a person he was, in every sense of the word.

I was initially drawn to Simon because of the languages he knew. In a former life I created Hebrew, Syriac, Ugaritic, and even Akkadian fonts for a foreign language word processor. Like many linguistic novices I was amazed by Simon's expertise in the wondrous worlds of ancient languages and cultures. I quickly came to admire his wisdom and refined judgment. I saw how funny he was, in his dry way. I appreciated his piano playing. I relished his marvelous stories about the good old days when he and his wife Sonia first came to this country, as I had done with my wife. I teased him whenever Australian convict colonists beat the English mother country at cricket or rugby and he gave as good as he got. We jointly arranged some dinner parties for people related to the British Empire. I wanted to call it the Post-Colonial Aftermath group but he thought that name reflected poorly on the food. One of my children remembers Simon, with great sadness, as the first person to take him seriously as a musician.

Many of you have fond memories of Simon like these. It is striking how deeply loved he was. Because this Sunday is the first anniversary of Simon's death, he has been on our minds in the preparation of today's service. And he has been my imagined spiritual companion as I have reflected on the theme of untimely death. Surely Simon's death was untimely. What shall we say about this?

In the face of existentially loaded issues such as untimely death, I instinctively reach for the Hebrew Bible's wisdom literature. As I read this passage from Ecclesiastes, I struggle to absorb its suggestion that everything has a proper time. No death is truly untimely, it says, but God sets the events of life in their place for God's own purposes, which are beyond our understanding.

I confess to feeling despair at this picture of God consciously regulating all events, inscrutably doing the divine thing no matter how you or I might feel about it. This is one of those places when I want to take the Bible seriously by fighting with it. Are we supposed to believe that Simon's death was divinely mandated? That our friends who bury their children are fulfilling a supernatural agenda? That 33 people at Virginia Tech died on God's schedule? That thousands of Americans and many times more Iraqis have died according to a heavenly timetable? That one million children die each month from needless hunger and avoidable disease because of the mercurial whims of God's administration? That the millions of past species filling the history of our ecosystem went extinct right on time? That the endless train of death that drives evolutionary emergence expresses the creative divine presence in our hapless and hopeless and heartless planet?

I can picture Simon trying to steady me as I get upset, but I am not finished. As if to Simon himself, I will confess to you that I cannot give my allegiance to a God who is consciously, personally aware of such prodigious piles of predators and prey, all propagating energy along toward the future in accordance with a special divine plan that is always right on time. At this point I have enormous sympathy with Christian Fundamentalists of the young-earth creationist type, who believe that God made everything in six days, a few thousand years ago, just like Genesis says. Despite their historical error, they understand the moral implications of evolutionary death far more clearly than their cavalier liberal brethren.

If I have to believe in God as a personal, aware, active creator, then I need an ancient worldview to match. I would gladly serve a God who creates the way Genesis hints, lovingly making each creature, fully formed, responsive to God's gift of life. If God has to be a big and powerful person, then give me Genesis or give me nothing! To hell with the countless death pits of our planetary history, to hell with the meandering experimentation of evolution, and to hell with coincidence and bad luck and pointless suffering and meaningless murder and being in the wrong place at the wrong time. In fact, to hell with untimely death. If God has to be a super-person who knows and cares and protects, then give me a world where evil acts of mass murder are never the outworking of mental illness and social torture but always simply the wicked deeds of bad people. Give me a God with a plan, even though I can't grasp its purpose. Give me Ecclesiastes!

I imagine Simon smiling at this point, wondering if I am finished with my rant and whether it is safe to intervene. He always took me seriously and I am sure in this case that he would remind me of his favorite Psalms. There we often read the poetry of people who don't understand what is happening to them. They reach out to God in praise and petition, and sometimes complain about injustice and beg God to please stop standing around and do something. Instead of falling into despair, they maintain a connection with God by making sure God knows that the divine timing doesn't suit them. David's complaining in the Psalms strikes me as self-serving at times, which is true for all of us, but he is made bold by friendship. The stranger would never be so rude as to complain in the divine presence. Only the one who knows God intimately as merciful friend would speak in such a way. There is such beautiful trust expressed in complaint to God.

If the Psalms teach us to complain when we just can't pretend with God that everything is OK, then Ecclesiastes adds another lesson: that we are pretty much in the dark about God's purposes. How could we know what is the final meaning of life, or what is the divine point in the twists and turns of our biographies? How could we know what God is up to at Virginia Tech or where the dead from that horrific day will go? Ecclesiastes says, "The fate of humans and the fate of animals is the same; as one dies, so dies the other. They all have the same breath . . . all are from the dust, and all turn to dust again. Who knows whether the human spirit goes upward and the spirit of animals goes downward to the earth?" (19–22).

How ignorant are we? Let me answer with a story. I work with teenagers at a local church. One of my charges recently told me a story about the mischief he and a playmate got up to one time. The two boys were probably three years old at the time. Their problem was to cut a very small and very precious slip of paper in half. Not finding any scissors, one of the kids tracked down a huge pair of hedge shears. Then, in their wobbly three-year-old way, one kid held up the tiny piece of paper and the other held up the appallingly sharp and menacing hedge shears and took aim. I don't have the heart to tell you precisely what happened next. I can say that, every time this young man plays the saxophone, I give thanks that skilled doctors were able to reattach the finger.

In the big questions of life, we are like these boys with their toys. We are vastly ignorant and extremely dangerous. We cause trouble without trying. Often enough we are part of the problem and just don't care, or else we feel helpless to make a difference. Sometimes we callously perpetrate great evil. The author of Ecclesiastes may be right: There is wickedness in the place of justice and we can't sort it out; humans are no different than complicated animals; all is vanity. If we are as ignorant as three-year-olds with hedge shears, then who are we to judge God's administration of the world?

The Ecclesiastes kind of humility produces patience and compassion. When joined with trusting Psalmic complaint, it defines an authentic spiritual path for people who think of God as a supernatural person, aware of everything that happens, and guiding all earthly events according to divine timing and purposes. On that path, the Virginia Tech killings must make sense on some scale unknown to us. The seemingly premature death of our colleagues Simon Parker and Prathia Hall and Tony Campbell and John Clayton come into meaningful focus through some lens that we do not possess. Even mass death of the poor must have a place in God's plan. There is no such thing as untimely death in Ecclesiastes, except as we judge it so in our desperate ignorance.

At this point, I imagine Simon staring at me, quietly wondering if I will leave the matter here, with the Ecclesiastes vision of human ignorance, divine supervision, and no truly untimely death. He would need to do nothing more than stare in order to force the question about whether I have told the truth, the whole truth, and nothing but the truth. I picture myself bleakly staring back at him for a while, before resolving to press deeper.

I already confessed that, if God has to be a super-person who knows and cares and acts on a timetable, then I need a Genesis worldview, or an Ecclesiastes worldview, to go with it. The biblical authors had such a world, but we do not. In the Ecclesiastes picture of events, everything has a season and God pays intimate attention to every detail because we are at the very center of things, in time, in space, and in God's consciousness.

How things have changed! Here are three philosophical cosmology lessons. Lesson #1: Biological evolution happens over a four-billion-year time scale, with over 99% of all Earth species now extinct. Human beings are late arrivals and will eventually be replaced by yet other species. We are not the culminating purpose of this world, even if we are a valuable part of it. Lesson #2: Cosmic evolution tells the wondrous story of a fourteen-billion-year expansion of the universe, full of exploding stars and creativity on every scale from sub-atomic particles to galaxy clusters. Indeed, contemporary cosmology appears to require countless universes more and less similar to ours. We are very far from being at the center of cosmic reality, even if we are profoundly special. Lesson #3: This universe is full of chances sparkling away within the constraints of nature's law-like regularities. This fertile interplay of chance and necessity creates cells and ecosystems, each with special value. Ants and plants and people live for a while and then return to the earth, feeding the future. This universe is not divinely scheduled but full of chances.

My difficulty accepting the Ecclesiastes picture of things is not the problem of suffering and God's goodness. The ancients had to contend with suffering and violence, as we do. They had to come to grips with apparently untimely death and pointless suffering, as we do and much worse than we do. The Ecclesiastes answer of humble trust is a profound one.

My difficulty is that the Ecclesiastes world matches the personality of the Ecclesiastes God, whereas my world does not. The big God in the Sky has become less believable to me not because the idea is intrinsically incoherent but because my understanding of the sky has changed. The cognitive dissonance between a loving, active, personal creator deity and the world we encounter today is painful to me. Mass murder and the premature death of friends just amplifies the dissonance. Most modern people sense this at some level. This is one of the challenges we all must navigate.

For religious leaders, the rubber meets the road when we have to speak in public about untimely death or crazed killings or stupid wars. Will you say with Ecclesiastes that there is a time for every purpose under heaven, and that God has everything under control even when we can't make sense of it? Can you honestly say that this is the deep meaning of Simon's death, of the Virginia Tech killings? What about brutal African wars in the aftermath of colonialism, or the European Holocaust?

Many theological liberals can't accept the Ecclesiastes line. They picture God not only as a personal being, as Ecclesiastes does, but also as a very nice person whose moral character should be transparently good, whereas Ecclesiastes assumes our ignorance in place of such transparency. They simply can't abide the idea of God having the power to intervene and yet doing nothing to stop a gunman from following a girl back to her dorm room and shooting her. They can't imagine God doing less than her dorm adviser did, who apparently tried to intervene and was also shot dead. They certainly can't picture a good God allowing the mass murder that followed. All it would have taken to change the situation was for the shooter to wake up with the flu, or to twist an ankle, or to meet a kind person who unknowingly breaks through his psychotic isolation. Couldn't God manage at least that much? How about a bolt of lightning?

Liberal theologians tie themselves in tortured knots at this point. They suppose that God can't intervene, and that's why nothing happens. If God did anything, they reason, then God would violate the autonomy of creation. If we want to do bad or crazy things, God has to let us. But do you think a parent would stand back and watch as one three-year-old sliced off the finger of another, on the basis that mothers and fathers should not infringe on the freedom of their children? Of course not! That would be parental neglect. Well, if God is a good personal creator being, if God is a parent who stands by as his ignorant children kill one another, then God is guilty of parental neglect also, guilty on a massive scale.

I confess to you that if God is this sort of creator, then I believe our goodness exceeds God's. We should spend our last breath resisting the heartless neglect of this divine monster. We should make untimely death our problem to solve and never trust God again.

At this point, I cannot picture what Simon would say. I know he possessed great sensitivity to questions of needless suffering and untimely death. But I do not know for sure how he resolved the issue in his own heart and mind. If there is a heaven and I am fortunate enough one day to share a heavenly beverage with Simon while watching angelic cricket beside him, I shall ask him how he would have advised me to conclude this sermon. For now, I simply speak from the heart.

The ancient idea of God as a personal being does not work for me spiritually or intellectually. But another ancient idea of God does work for me. This idea pictures God not as a supernatural personal being but as the Ground of Being—the depth structures of nature and the wellsprings of value. We engage this God with every part of our bodies and minds in every circumstance. This God is neither personal nor anti-personal but the very condition for the possibility of everything that is. This includes personal beings like us, and also the impersonal and unguided exploration of possibilities that so much of the universe expresses. Just as we sprang from spontaneous divine creativity, so we return into the divine abyss when we die. Union with this God is less like me watching a game of cricket with Simon and more like a dew drop slipping silently into the shining sea.

I suspect that some of you could never be Christians if this idea of God as Ground of Being had to be your constant companion, your finest hope and greatest love. In that case, you know what to say about untimely death: steer clear of tortured explanations of divine silence and go with Ecclesiastes. Our pain and grief is a side effect of our ignorance. If we could see as God sees we would not be so unhinged by tragedy. As it is, we must trust that personal divine creator remains in final control of everything that happens, and that there is no such thing as untimely death.

That is an honorable path but it is not my path. I remain a Christian in the face of untimely death because the idea of God as Ground of Being hovers within the Christian tradition, fueling and deepening it, often from its underside. Each of us is on our own journey toward death, and we are profoundly ignorant about ultimate matters. But sometimes we must take a stand. Here is where I stand. On the long path toward ultimate silence in the divine presence, my guide is Jesus Christ, whom I follow, and my God is no supernatural personal creator but the pulsing heart of the depths of reality, which I love.

I am not sure but I suspect Simon would gently disagree with me. Perhaps he would defend the Ecclesiastes vision: patient submission to the creator God of implacable timetables and impenetrable purposes. But perhaps Ecclesiastes and I have more in common than it appears. Ironically, as I ponder God as the Ground of Being, Ecclesiastes comes alive for me again. There is a time for every purpose under heaven. It is not the timing of an aware and active divine being who takes some people while sparing others, according to some inscrutable divine purpose that directs a gunman to one classroom rather than another. No, it is the timing of reality itself, in which we live and move and have our being, in which we dance along with the rhythms of nature, in which we survive according to the chances of good and bad fortune.

We can suffer randomly and it is still meaningful because it is God's suffering as well as ours. We can catch a nasty disease or have an unlucky accident, and dying is still divinely blessed. We can be in the wrong place at the wrong time, at the mercy of a murderous mind, and it is still God's time for us to die. Ecclesiastes lives again, in an updated worldview and with a different idea of God. Now even untimely death has its season. A divine being may not schedule it. And we may not like it if we can glimpse it rushing toward us. But death is always sacred because it ushers in our return to the Ground of our Being, our return to the heart of God, our return home.

God Is . . . Creator

READINGS

O Lord, our Sovereign,
>how majestic is your name in all the earth!

You have set your glory above the heavens.
>Out of the mouths of babes and infants

you have founded a bulwark because of your foes,
>to silence the enemy and the avenger.

When I look at your heavens, the work of your fingers,
>the moon and the stars that you have established;

what are human beings that you are mindful of them,
>mortals that you care for them?

Yet you have made them a little lower than God,
>and crowned them with glory and honour.

You have given them dominion over the works of your hands;
>you have put all things under their feet,

all sheep and oxen,
>and also the beasts of the field,

the birds of the air, and the fish of the sea,
>whatever passes along the paths of the seas.

O Lord, our Sovereign,
>how majestic is your name in all the earth!
>>PSALM 8

Then the Lord answered Job out of the whirlwind:
"Who is this that darkens counsel by words without knowledge?
Gird up your loins like a man,
  I will question you, and you shall declare to me.
"Where were you when I laid the foundation of the earth?
  Tell me, if you have understanding.
Who determined its measurements—surely you know!
  Or who stretched the line upon it?
On what were its bases sunk,
  or who laid its cornerstone
when the morning stars sang together
  and all the heavenly beings shouted for joy?"
    JOB 38:1–7

In the beginning was the Word, and the Word was with God, and the Word was God. He was in the beginning with God. All things came into being through him, and without him not one thing came into being. What has come into being in him was life, and the life was the light of all people. The light shines in the darkness, and the darkness did not overcome it.

JOHN 1:1–5

MEDITATION

I consider myself an evangelical Christian of the liberal sort, but I have many evangelical Christian relatives, friends, and students who are extremely conservative. Despite mutual respect, it appears that I have little in common with them, theologically. My outlook on life and faith leaves me feeling dismayed by what strikes me as their doctrinal and moral rigidity, appalled by their dismissal of the wisdom of other religions, and a little frightened by their willingness to vest absolute authority in an allegedly plain reading of the Bible. But my self-righteous theological appraisal does not go unchallenged. From their point of view, I am disloyal to what they see as the supernaturally established tradition of the Christian faith, dangerously cavalier about the fragile moral fabric of society, and all too willing to besmirch the purity of divine revelation with arrogant reliance on human reason and experience. They wouldn't hesitate to declare, with relief, that they share little in common, theologically, with me.

At the personal level, this liberal-conservative difference is manageable, so long as we don't have to resolve disagreements about biblical authority, so long as we care for one another, and so long as we remember to laugh at ourselves from time to time. At the cultural level, however, the liberal-conservative difference has the proportions of an unbridgeable chasm, which makes it seem deadly serious. Often enough it is a hateful and deadly disagreement. The murder of late-term abortion provider Dr. George Tiller inside the Reformation Lutheran Church of Wichita, Kansas, as he prepared to welcome worshippers into the sanctuary and talked with a friend about taking his grandchildren to Disney World shows how deadly the disagreement can become. And there are many other disastrous consequences of religious hatred.

Most fundamentalist and conservative evangelical groups decried Dr. Tiller's murder but others, such as Rev. Fred Phelps' Westboro Baptist Church, said Dr. Tiller got what he deserved and even picketed his funeral. Meanwhile, the violent rhetoric that inspires extremists to act out their distorted heroic fantasies continues. Sometimes it seems that the United States is only a small step away from the religious violence that has been so disastrous between Catholics and Protestants in Ireland, or between Sunnis and Shiites in the Middle East.

Such disagreements among religious people are sad and strange, in some ways. After all, we do have a great deal in common, including our love of children, our celebration of our mothers and fathers, our preference for peaceful neighborhoods, our quest for health and happiness, and our conviction that life is best lived in relation to an ultimate reality that suffuses everyday events and transcends everyday concerns. But despite these shared life goals, mutual suspicion and hostility are very real.

My focus here is on one front of the disagreement, namely, the evolution wars—more specifically, we'll skip past the wider secular-versus-religious debate over evolution and zoom in on the form the dispute takes among Christian believers, most of whom accept that the world is God's creation and thereafter have to figure out whether and how to incorporate evolutionary theory into that basic conviction. I hope to demonstrate that each group of Christians has something valuable to learn from the other. As far as I know, the evolution controversy has not produced fanatical murders. But it continues to be extremely painful and it surfaces the substantive disagreements clearly.

※

The dispute among Christians over the theological implications of evolution arises on the back of four deeper disagreements.

First, we have conflicting visions of reality. The conservative evangelical imaginative world is defined by a God who knows the world intimately, who cares about each one of us personally, who acts freely according to divine purposes, and who answers our prayers in fatherly love when we ask in confident faith. The liberal evangelical imaginative world is defined by a God who is beyond measure and understanding, speaking from the whirlwind of creativity in ways that are sometimes difficult to comprehend. One God is scaled to human needs and interests and sits awkwardly with evolution, while the other is vastly beyond every worldly agenda, and suits evolution more naturally.

Second, we have conflicting visions of authority. The conservative evangelical vests authority in definitive divine revelation, expressed decisively through the Bible, the Pope, or some other religious touchstone. The liberal evangelical vests authority in traditions of interpretation, accepting diversity, contradictions, and struggles within those traditions as unavoidable and valuable. If evolution contradicts the authoritative revelation of the nature of God then evolution is easily rejected for one side, whereas the other side naturally seeks a creative synthesis.

Third, we have conflicting visions of history. The conservative evangelical regards culture and civilization and scientific discovery as the ambiguous stage for the drama of salvation but never salvific in itself, and always subordinate to theological truth. The liberal evangelical sees history as a process of development that can be appreciated as part of what salvation means, and thus as able to challenge traditionally received religious beliefs. One side has little reason to respect scientific theories such as evolution if they contradict revealed truth, whereas the other side receives evolution as a magnificent divine revelation about the world that must be taken seriously no matter what traditional theology says.

Finally, we have conflicting visions of church. The conservative evangelical sees correctness of doctrine as a vital form of religious purity, and will sacrifice church unity to protect it—by expelling those who stubbornly resist the party line, if necessary. Meanwhile, the liberal evangelical tries hard to tolerate doctrinal variations because certainty about such matters is impossible, and because unity of believers matters more than purity of beliefs. One side handles tension between God-beliefs and evolution by rejecting evolution to protect doctrinal purity, while the other side minimizes the tension in the name of Christian unity and in hopes that God-beliefs and evolution can somehow be reconciled.

For the sake of clarity, I should plainly acknowledge my view that conservative evangelicals who reject evolution in favor of creationism, or who embrace the neo-creationism of Intelligent Design theory, make a serious error in judgment. Yet they understand what is theologically at stake in evolution far better than most of their liberal counterparts who casually resolve the issue by declaring that God creates through evolution, without pausing to think through what that must mean.

Charles Darwin, whose two-hundredth birthday we celebrate this year, began his scholarly career as a convinced believer that God intentionally conceived, designed, and created the world in roughly the form Darwin encountered it. As a young man he read and accepted the still-famous design arguments of his countryman William Paley. After all, he couldn't explain the wondrous structure of the eye any other way; he had to assume a personal, benevolent, attentive, and active designer God. As his studies widened and deepened, however, Darwin's theological views slowly shifted. Though he never discovered the DNA mechanism by which traits were transmitted across generations, he was confident that trait preservation and transmission occur, and that random variations of traits make organisms more and less fit to survive the rigors of any given environment. He believed that this process of trait inheritance, random variation, and natural selection in competitive environments is powerful enough to explain the origin of species, which is the name he gave to his most famous book, published 150 years ago. And he assembled a formidable array of evidence to support his theory—evidence that is extraordinarily difficult to explain apart from the evolutionary hypothesis.

Unsurprisingly, Darwin's view of God changed as the secrets of the natural world opened before his uncanny gaze. God was no longer necessary to explain the particulars of the world and its teeming life forms. Rather, God's domain was the creation of the potentialities of the world-as-a-whole, a world that answered to the description that the theory of evolution provided. Unsurprisingly, to Darwin, God gradually seemed less personal, benevolent, attentive, and active. Surely such a loving, personal deity would have created in another way, a way that involved less trial and error, fewer false starts, less mindless chance, fewer tragic species extinctions, less dependence on random symbiotic collaborations, fewer pointless cruelties, and less reliance on predation to sort out the fit from the unfit. Darwin arguably never lost his faith in God. Rather, believing that God created through the evolutionary process, his growing knowledge of that process dramatically transformed his view of God. And this left him ill-at-ease with the anthropomorphic personal theism of his day, and with friends and colleagues who believed in a personal, benevolent, attentive, and active divine being.

Christians and other theists who casually assert that God creates through evolution—as if there is no theological problem with this—should pause and consider Darwin's faith journey. Darwin was theologically more perceptive than many of his liberal endorsers. He knew that saying God creates through evolution puts enormous stress on belief in a personal, benevolent, attentive, and active deity. Evolution casts a pall over the moral clarity that most people want to see in the God they worship and serve. Darwin felt the difficulty acutely. Many theologians since Darwin have struggled with the problem. But I think many people don't sense the challenge and casually blend evolutionary theory and belief in a personal, benevolent, attentive, and active God as if there is no problem.

Many of my conservative evangelical Christian brothers and sisters who reject evolutionary theory feel the problem Darwin felt. They instinctively grasp that their personal, benevolent, attentive, and active God could not possibly have created the world as Darwin described it. Such a God would be morally unrecognizable to them, a kind of heartless gambler over the lives and wellbeing of Earth's creatures, and not at all like the loving and wise parent they trust and serve. This would contradict their morally clear and homey worldview, which is borne up by a God of pure compassion and perfect goodness. Because they take on authority the proposition that God is personal, benevolent, attentive, and active, they know with confidence that Darwin must have been wrong.

To see the power of this argument, consider C. S. Lewis's creation story. It is in a lesser known volume of his Narnia Chronicles called *The*

Magician's Nephew. The children in that story are present when the great lion Aslan creates Narnia and its creatures. The method of creation is beautifully intimate and personal: Aslan sings in a majestic voice, with spectacularly complex undertones and rippling overtones, and the world awakens around him. Each creature struggles up and out of the Narnian soil, awakening to a new world, personally called into being by the fatherly lion God himself. I find the story enormously moving. You see, C. S. Lewis grasped the point that Darwin also felt so forcefully: the God Lewis believed in could not create in a way much different than Aslan did. Good literature is able to test the coherence of the "God creates through evolution" idea. So long as God is conceived as a personal, benevolent, attentive, and active being, like Aslan, the literary acid test shows that God cannot and would not create through evolution. They just don't fit.

Conservative evangelical Christians who resist evolutionary theory for theological reasons are shrewdly targeting a problem for their God-infused worldview, perhaps the sharpest problem that worldview has ever faced. They are not tiptoeing around, pretending that the God they trust every day somehow creates through evolution. They feel the contradiction and just say no to evolution. I admire that. I, too, feel the dilemma they feel. Since a personal, benevolent, attentive, and active deity cannot create through evolution, either that God or evolution must go. Unlike them, however, I am not in any doubt about the exceptional robustness of the theory of evolution. It is as stable a scientific theory as the atomic theory of matter.

For me, therefore, the choice leads to a different conclusion: God the creator simply cannot be a personal, benevolent, attentive, and active deity. We can preserve those affirmations symbolically and poetically but they do not refer to a divine being with intentions and awareness, with feelings and intelligence, with plans and powers to act. Rather, they refer to the Ground of Being itself, to the creative and fecund power source in the depths of nature, to the value structures and potentialities that the world manifests. They refer to the God beyond God, which is to say the truly ultimate reality that hovers behind and beneath and beyond the symbolic Gods we create and deploy to satisfy our personal needs, to make sense of our world, and to legitimate the exercise of social control.

You may be surprised to hear me praising the theological perceptiveness of the conservative evangelical resistance to evolutionary theory while also praising evolutionary theory itself. And you may be taken aback by my affirmation of the God beyond God, with the associated critique of more popular views of God as a personal, benevolent, attentive, and active being. I don't seek to convince you to agree with me about God; I understand this to be a bit of a stretch for most people. Rather, my aim is to convince you that there is a big problem trying to fit popular personal theism together with evolutionary theory—a bigger problem than many Christian believers and even many theologians are ready to admit. Ironically, it is the conservative evangelicals who resist evolutionary theory that really grasp this point. They believe in a God who could only create the world in something like the way Aslan creates Narnia. But Darwin showed us a different world. That revelation demands not atheism—not for Darwin and not for us today either—but a different conception of the divine. You may not think it is necessary to embrace my solution to this problem, but I am confident that we will never understand the real passion and coherence of the religious anti-evolution position until we grasp the problem that evolutionary theory poses for personal theism.

The luminous Narnian creation story helps to confirm what evolutionary theory shows us, namely, that God did not create that way. It also helps us grasp why a personal, benevolent, attentive, and active divine being could not and would not create through evolution. One of the readings has God interrogate Job, "Where were you when I laid the foundation of the earth?" Well, we were nowhere to be found, so we have to approach these matters with humility. But that does not mean we should be casual in our theological reasoning. The readings from Psalm 8 and John's Gospel set examples for us of careful thinking about the meaning of creation, and we should do the same. Conservative evangelical anti-evolutionists and neo-creationist Intelligent Design believers detect the inconsistency and are willing to protect their homey worldview at any cost—even if it means rejecting a scientific theory as well supported as evolutionary theory and the attendant migration into a cultural backwater where people who don't get what is at stake make fun of them.

It is genuinely difficult to be careful and consistent in this area. Most of us believe in a God who would and could create the world in the way Aslan created Narnia. But such a God could not and would not and did not create the world evolutionary theory shows us. And that presents a severe puzzle. When God speaks to us from the evolutionary whirlwind, do we hear a personal, benevolent, attentive, and active divine being addressing

God Is . . . Creator

us, soul to soul? Or do we hear the abysmal Ground of Being rumbling in fecund creativity, morally impenetrable, imponderably beautiful, and defying rational grasp? My spirituality is tuned to the latter conception, to the God beyond all Gods, so I can afford to acknowledge the theological perceptiveness of my conservative evangelical anti-evolutionist brothers and sisters. But personal theists who accept evolutionary biology must confront the question of what sort of God could, would, and did create the world through evolution.

Darwin faced this question squarely, and it haunted him; we should do no less. To the God who speaks to us from the whirlwind, demanding to know where we were when the foundations of the earth were laid, we owe our very best efforts to absorb what is revealed to us about the world we inhabit and to incorporate that into our faith journeys as honestly and consistently as we can.

God Is... Waiting

READINGS

Comfort, O comfort my people, says your God.

Speak tenderly to Jerusalem, and cry to her that she has served her term, that her penalty is paid, that she has received from the Lord's hand double for all her sins.

A voice cries out: "In the wilderness prepare the way of the LORD, make straight in the desert a highway for our God.

Every valley shall be lifted up, and every mountain and hill be made low; the uneven ground shall become level, and the rough places a plain.

Then the glory of the LORD shall be revealed, and all people shall see it together, for the mouth of the LORD has spoken."

A voice says, "Cry out!" And I said, "What shall I cry?" All people are grass, their constancy is like the flower of the field.

The grass withers, the flower fades, when the breath of the LORD blows upon it; surely the people are grass.

The grass withers, the flower fades; but the word of our God will stand forever.

Get you up to a high mountain, O Zion, herald of good tidings; lift up your voice with strength, O Jerusalem, herald of good tidings, lift it up, do not fear; say to the cities of Judah, "Here is your God!"

See, the Lord GOD comes with might, and his arm rules for him; his reward is with him, and his recompense before him.

He will feed his flock like a shepherd; he will gather the lambs in his arms, and carry them in his bosom, and gently lead the mother sheep.

ISAIAH 40:1–11

God Is . . . Waiting

LORD, you were favorable to your land; you restored the fortunes of Jacob.

You forgave the iniquity of your people; you pardoned all their sin. Selah

Let me hear what God the LORD will speak, for he will speak peace to his people, to his faithful, to those who turn to him in their hearts.

Surely his salvation is at hand for those who fear him, that his glory may dwell in our land.

Steadfast love and faithfulness will meet; righteousness and peace will kiss each other.

Faithfulness will spring up from the ground, and righteousness will look down from the sky.

The LORD will give what is good, and our land will yield its increase.

Righteousness will go before him, and will make a path for his steps.

PSALM 85:1–2, 8–13

But do not ignore this one fact, beloved, that with the Lord one day is like a thousand years, and a thousand years are like one day.

The Lord is not slow about his promise, as some think of slowness, but is patient with you, not wanting any to perish, but all to come to repentance.

But the day of the Lord will come like a thief, and then the heavens will pass away with a loud noise, and the elements will be dissolved with fire, and the earth and everything that is done on it will be disclosed.

Since all these things are to be dissolved in this way, what sort of persons ought you to be in leading lives of holiness and godliness,

waiting for and hastening the coming of the day of God, because of which the heavens will be set ablaze and dissolved, and the elements will melt with fire?

But, in accordance with his promise, we wait for new heavens and a new earth, where righteousness is at home.

Therefore, beloved, while you are waiting for these things, strive to be found by him at peace, without spot or blemish;

and regard the patience of our Lord as salvation. So also our beloved brother Paul wrote to you according to the wisdom given him.

2 PETER 3:8–15A

The beginning of the good news of Jesus Christ, the Son of God.

As it is written in the prophet Isaiah, "See, I am sending my messenger ahead of you, who will prepare your way;

the voice of one crying out in the wilderness: 'Prepare the way of the Lord, make his paths straight.'"

John the baptizer appeared in the wilderness, proclaiming a baptism of repentance for the forgiveness of sins.

And people from the whole Judean countryside and all the people of Jerusalem were going out to him, and were baptized by him in the river Jordan, confessing their sins.

Now John was clothed with camel's hair, with a leather belt around his waist, and he ate locusts and wild honey.

He proclaimed, "The one who is more powerful than I is coming after me; I am not worthy to stoop down and untie the thong of his sandals.

I have baptized you with water; but he will baptize you with the Holy Spirit."

MARK 1:1–8

MEDITATION

There are two kinds of waiting. The readings for today amply testify to both, and also offer shadowy hints at a third.

To begin with, there is the waiting with anticipation of joy, as when young children become irrepressibly excited about the arrival of Christmas. It's the music and colors and smells, the food and fun and family. Most of all it's the gifts, brought by the symbol of this kind of waiting: Father Christmas.

This is the way we often think of Advent: we just know something good and true and beautiful, something joyously world-changing, is right around the corner. The passages from Isaiah and Mark are shot through with the joy of excited expectation: the entire cosmos is on the edge of its seat waiting in anticipation for this life-changing moment!

Our enthusiasm for Advent might be more muted than young children approaching Christmas, because we are way too cool to get all effervescently happy, giggling and shrieking with excitement. But in our own more sedate ways, when the right hymn moves us or that special song reminds us, when we pick out that just-right gift for a special someone or decorate our favorite space, we too feel ourselves waiting for unbridled joy to be unveiled in its fullness.

In case we find ourselves jaded about ritual repetition of the Advent process of waiting, there is even a class of Advent sermons devoted to helping us remember how to be joyfully mindful. Those sermons teach us to avoid being sucked into the acquisitive vortex of commercialism, and they warn us about the black hole of endless Advent busyness. From either location, the true light of profound joy is impossible to discern.

This is not one of those sermons but you're likely to hear at least one this Advent season.

The weird thing about ritual repetition of waiting for the joyous event of Christmas is that we are not actually waiting for the original joyous event to occur. After all, the One Christians follow, Jesus who is called the Christ, was born long ago, at an unknown time of year, having uncertain parentage and bleak prospects. We remember the baby Jesus because of the stunning impact the grown-up Jesus had on his followers, and that is an excellent reason to celebrate that birth from long, long ago, regardless of when in the year it actually happened, and despite the difficulty of discerning its true conditions through the mists of time and legend.

If the event that Advent waiting ritually memorializes has already occurred, what is there to get personally excited about? What joy are we waiting for?

There is another whole class of Advent sermons devoted to explaining that we are actually waiting for the arrival of Jesus the Christ in our hearts and minds. In those sermons, Advent is about the annual intensification of awareness that God is present in our world despite appearances, that we are in God's hands despite our hesitancy to trust, and that Jesus' life and example is always there for us to follow, if we so choose.

This is not one of those sermons, either, but if you pay attention you are bound to hear that message from the pulpit at some point this Advent season.

God Is . . .

In my experience, waiting for the manifestation of joy is a fragile thing. I savor my children's pure delight in the wonder of Father Christmas partly because I know what's coming: along with the triumphs and happiness there will be the inevitable collapse of life dreams, the failures of character in the face of everyday challenges, and the moments of tragedy and pain—in short, the ordinary frustration and finitude of life. The imagined nativity scene of the baby Jesus evokes his terrible fate. His mother's joy at his birth is darkly pervaded by her cries of despairing helplessness at her son's execution. The harsh realities of life experience mock the expectation of pure, unbridled joy as a delusional state of mind—a transitional emotion to be enjoyed, perhaps, but never to be trusted as a reliable sign of the nature of our world.

Knowing this, as each one of us does from our intimately personal experiences of the ambiguity of life, it is possible to yield to despair. We can easily surrender to a vision of the dark talons of life wrapped around the gleaming face of every child whose eyes are lit up with delight. After all, there is another kind of waiting, a darker kind.

This second kind of waiting is waiting in dread.

We can wait in dread because we know what's coming. We wait in dread, certain that most of our malnourished children will die before they reach five years of age in a bizarre lottery of fate. We wait in dread, knowing that our torturer will return to drive us into unimaginable pain. We wait in dread for the next incident of racist brutality or homophobic cruelty or sexual violence.

We can also wait in dread because we don't know what's coming. We wait in dread, not knowing whether our species will navigate the rapid climate change we are helping to cause. We wait in dread, not knowing whether religious zealots will gain control of the weapons of mass destruction they need to bring the human world to an end through a fiery nuclear dénouement or through a nightmare of twisted biotech wizardry. We wait in dread, not knowing whether our immune systems will be able to manage the cancerous cells that are always forming within our bodies, or whether our minds and memories will dissolve in the devastating haze of dementia or psychiatric illness.

Advent, properly understood, is a time of waiting in dread. This is partly because we know what happened to the baby Jesus; witness the holy-land nativity scene where the baby Jesus is depicted with cruciform limbs and wearing a crown of thorns. And it is partly because we don't know what will happen to us, whether God will be present to us as absence, as impenetrable holy mystery, or as friend and companion on serendipitous paths.

Waiting in dread can paralyze us. In the most severe circumstances, when injustice and violence rain down like acid from the sky and surge around us like poisonous flood waters, no other kind of waiting is possible.

Often enough, though, we can win through to a kind of acceptance of the lurking dangers, known and unknown. We can remember that "All people are grass, their constancy is like the flower of the field. The grass withers, the flower fades, when the breath of the LORD blows upon it."

In its higher forms, this acceptance is no mere cognitive recognition of the ambiguity and pain of life. Rather, it is a wholehearted spiritual surrender. It is, quite literally, wanting our lives to be exactly where they most truly are: in the hands of God, for whom "one day is like a thousand years, and a thousand years are like one day," who comes like a thief in the night to destroy everything under heaven and also to "gather the lambs in his arms."

To surrender to God in this way is to see God in all our waiting, even when we wait in dread because of what we know and what we don't know. To stay in this place of holy surrender is to trust as a lamb trusts in the arms of the shepherd. In this way, despite all worldly indications to the contrary, waiting in dread can evoke waiting for joy—the simple joy of acceptance, the resonant joy of wonder, the happy joy of belonging, and the spiritually potent joy of discipleship.

And so we complete the cycle, from waiting for joy to waiting in dread and back to waiting in joy, deepened and refined by warranted dread, which itself is festooned with the sparkling ribbons of celebration. As the cycle rolls ever onwards, we begin to lose track of which is which, as dread and joy merge into a symphony of wonder, of wistfulness, of worship. In that blessed state of awareness, we see the Alpha and the Omega joined in an everlasting circle, waiting merging with remembering, dread with joy, the Christ-child with the executed prisoner, divine presence with divine absence.

Oddly enough, it is in this merged state of wonder that we discern the hint of another kind of Advent waiting. It is difficult to detect this waiting because it is masked by the mist of human pain and longing. But in the merged state of wonder, where joy blends with dread in our waiting, our eyes are lifted above our own concerns in worship, and there it is: God is waiting, too. God is in our waiting, whether joyful or dreadful, but God also waits, for us and for all things to manifest their potential, to make their choices, to realize some possibilities and foreclose others.

The God of waiting is not a busy agent pushing the world hither and yon, prodding, chastising, intervening, or luring us toward anything in particular. Rather, this God is the very Ground of Being, the depth structures and dynamic flows of life, the cosmic Dao and the God beyond God of our beloved mystics. This God waits for the unfolding of nature itself, of our very lives.

If this God had feelings, I imagine there would be both joy and dread in the divine waiting. There would be joy in achieved harmonies of emergent complexity and dread in awaiting the inevitable entropic dispersal of those harmonies as they are reclaimed by chaos. God would wait in dread for the manifestation of our own failures of character, for our obliviousness to the pain of others to mushroom into the disasters of structural evil, for our fear to hold us back from making the most of this precious gift of life. And God would wait in joy for the forging of Christ-like virtues in our own lives, for every moment in which we follow Jesus' example and tie our personal energy and safety to the fates of the defenseless, for our courage to blossom into beautiful justice that rolls down like waters from heaven.

Dear friends on the Way, during Advent, let us wait with the irrepressible joy of childlike wonder. Let us accept that we must wait in dread for the failure of our hopes and the arrival of tragedy. Let us wait with our mystical brothers and sisters in that wondrous state of surrender where joy bespeaks dread and dread is shot through with joy, in that potent state that lifts our eyes above our pain and pleasure into worship of the Holy One. And let us wait mindful that God, also, waits for us.

www.ingramcontent.com/pod-product-compliance
Lightning Source LLC
Chambersburg PA
CBHW022117090426
42743CB00008B/895